Run · Jump · Hide · Slide · Splash

Run · Jump · Hide · Slide · Splash
The 200 Best Outdoor Games Ever

Joe Rhatigan &
Rain Newcomb

LARK BOOKS
A Division of Sterling Publishing Co., Inc.
New York

This book is dedicated to Tommy (Yo, Bro!), Ellen, Diane, Kim, Greg, Keith, Mike, Loretta, Eileen, Gina, Donna, Laurie, Patrick, Andrea, Cookie, and all the other kids who played on Avenue M between 45th and 46th.
--JR

For Erik O. Johnson, who invented the game Soft Fuzzy Things of Death so that I wouldn't keep getting hit in the face with the dodge ball during gym class.
--RN

Art Director: Tom Metcalf
Associate Art Director: Shannon Yokeley
Photographer: Sandra Stambaugh
Cover Designer: Barbara Zaretsky
Illustrator: Orrin Lundgren
Editorial Assistance: Delores Gosnell
Editorial Interns: Robin Heimer and Rebecca Lim
Art Intern: Sharease Curl

10 9 8 7 6 5 4 3 2 1

First Edition

Published by Lark Books, A Division of
Sterling Publishing Co., Inc.
387 Park Avenue South, New York, N.Y. 10016

© 2004, Lark Books

Distributed in Canada by Sterling Publishing,
c/o Canadian Manda Group, One Atlantic Ave., Suite 105
Toronto, Ontario, Canada M6K 3E7

Distributed in the U.K. by Guild of Master Craftsman Publications Ltd., Castle Place,
166 High Street, Lewes, East Sussex, England
BN7 1XU
Tel: (+ 44) 1273 477374, Fax: (+ 44) 1273 478606, Email: pubs@thegmcgroup.com,
Web: www.gmcpublications.com

Distributed in Australia by Capricorn Link (Australia) Pty Ltd.,
P.O. Box 704, Windsor, NSW 2756 Australia

If you have questions or comments about this book, please contact:
Lark Books
67 Broadway
Asheville, NC 28801
(828) 253-0467
Manufactured in China

ISBN 1-57990-509-9

Acknowledgments

Thank you to all the people who helped make this book possible, especially:

Our art director Tom Metcalf, who made sure the kids were having a good time and worked hard to make this book beautiful and fun.

Our photographer Sandra Stambaugh, who got wherever she needed to be to make sure she got the perfect shot every time.

The awesome kids who played hard, had fun, and taught us some great new games (which are in this book!):

Fletcher Dale Armstrong
Chance Barry
Alexander Burt
Benjamin Burt
Aja Annette Cobbs
Betty Cobbs
Devon Dickerson
Sara Liu Eichelberger
Haley Jo Haynes
Jacob Katz
Olivia Kopp
Barcley Michelle Boyd
James Bailey Boyd
Jacob Douglas Hill
Nicholas Daniel Hill
Christopher Lee Hewitt
Natalie Elizabeth Hewitt
Olivia S.B. Kieffer
Margaret Ann Lasher
Mary Kathryn Lasher
Terrance Micahel Lonergan
Daniel M. Luna
Corrina Matthews
Aidan McKinney
Austin Meminger
Emerson Taylor Moorhead

Natasha Marie Perez
Niroshka Perez
Samuel Patrick Rardin
Thomas Taylor
Anna Meili Weshener-Dunning
Tobie Grace Meigian Weshrer
Reid Yanik
Ryan William Yanik

Thank you to the parents, for sharing your delightful children with us, and to Mr. and Ms. Tamasovich for letting us play in your pool.

And thanks especially to Dana Boyd, for helping out and always showing up with food. You're a Supermom!

Contents

Introduction

"What do you want to do?"
"I don't know. What do YOU want to do?"
"I don't know..."

Ever have a conversation like this with a friend or two? Sure you have. There you all are sitting around outside on a beautiful day because your mom threatened to find **something** for you to do if you couldn't think of something. And you know full well that what mom finds for you to do will be work and not fun. I mean, here you are with all the time in the world, a few friends hanging around, and you've got NOTHING TO DO! Well, never fear. *Run, Jump, Hide, Slide, Splash* is here to the rescue. Never again will you find yourself wishing school would hurry up and start. Never again will you have to dust your dad's commemorative fishing lures because you couldn't think of anything better to do. This book will test your abilities, your cunning, your smarts, and so many other skills you didn't even know you had. AND YOU WILL HAVE FUN. We promise.

This book is chock full of awesome outdoor games to play. We've included classics your parents will remember playing back in the Stone Ages. We've got new games that will have you wishing the day would never end. So, the next time you get stuck with the I-don't-know-what-do-you-want-to-do blues, find a game, read the rules, grab a friend (or two, or four, or five, or eight) and any stuff you might need, and give it a try.

Don't like that game? Try one of the other 199 we've included. You'll find games to play in the yard, at the park, on the sidewalk, in a field, or in the pool. Some you can play just about anywhere.

The games are listed in alphabetical order, and you can check out the indexes starting on page 126 if you're looking to play certain kinds of games, such as water games, games with balls, or games needing only two people, and more. Ready? Let's play.

A Note to Parents

My grandfather was a great games person, and he passed along the love of games to my father. I can recall many summers when my dad would get the neighborhood kids together for a summer-long Olympics. Every evening, right after dinner, we'd play a game or two. We played handball, roly poly, horse, man hunt, hit the penny, freeze tag, and even stick ball. We always planned on keeping score and calculating at the end of the summer who won the most games. We never did. The gold medal winner was supposed to win a free "Kitchen Sink" (which included every kind of ice cream imaginable with piles of sprinkles, melted fudge, and other extras on top) at the local Jahn's ice cream parlor. We were all winners the moment we dug in with giant spoons and appetites. And even without the ice cream we were all winners.

We played hard; we played fair (most of the time); and we formed friendships that lasted years. I don't remember who won more games of stoopball. I just remember playing stoopball.

I wrote this book with Rain not only to celebrate the glorious past of playing games in neighborhoods, but also to share these games with the next generation of players—kids whose parents are beginning to realize that not every second of their kids' lives has to be filled with a planned activity.

Neighborhood sidewalks, parks, and backyards are filling up again with kids whose appointment books are not quite as jam packed with soccer practice, music lessons, and art camps. (Hey, don't get me wrong; those things are great too!) And they're ready to play. Don't be timid. Join in the fun. And don't forget the ice cream.

Joe

A Few Things You Might Want to Know

Check out some of the following ideas on how to make the game you're playing even more fun for everyone.

Setting Up Boundaries

Some of the games in this book require boundaries to be set up. The size of the boundaries depends on how many people are playing the game. There should be enough room for everyone to run around without crashing into each other (too much). If you find that your IT can't tag anyone out, make the boundaries smaller. If IT can tag everyone in seven seconds, make the boundaries larger.

* **Use fences, sidewalks, trees, and walls to mark the boundaries.**

* **Use chalk to draw boundaries on sidewalks and other paved surfaces.**

* **Use rope, plastic cones, rocks, or extra shirts to mark boundaries in grass.**

* **Draw invisible lines between two fixed points (like a tree and the edge of the house) to be the boundaries.**

Balls and Other Equipment

Some of the games in this book suggest that you use a particular ball or piece of equipment. If you don't have the exact piece of equipment but still want to play the game, how about trying it with something else? For instance, if you want to play stickball but only have a dodge ball, try playing with that. As long as your stick or bat doesn't break the first time you hit the dodge ball with it, you've got a new version of stickball!

Choosing Teams

There are many ways to pick teams. Here are just a couple:

* **Line up and count off, so that every player says "one" or "two." The ones are all on one team, and the twos are on the other. You can line up in any order, or you can line up according to something, such as age, shirt color, or alphabetical order.**

* **Pick a captain for each team. The captains take turns picking players to be on their teams.**

Choosing Referees

Some times you may need a referee. If you do, see if somebody wants to volunteer. Sometimes somebody's tired and needs a little break from the game but still wants to be involved: Hello, ref!

If you've got extra players waiting their turn to play, have them referee. You can also try to find a friendly adult to referee for you. If no one wants to referee, choose someone using any of the Choosing IT methods on the next page, and decide how you'll rotate players so that everybody gets to play for a while.

Choosing IT

There are lots of ways to pick IT. Here are several:

✳ **Call "Not IT!" The last player to call "Not IT" is IT. You can also do something like touch your nose when saying "Not IT."**

✳ **Run a race. The last person to finish is IT.**

✳ **Tear up pieces of paper and mark one with an X, or use pennies that all have the same year except one. Put them in a hat and have every one pick one. The person who gets the odd penny or X is IT.**

✳ **Use counting rhymes. Stand in a circle and chant one of the following rhymes. One player points at each player (including himself) on every word. The person who is pointed at on the last word of the rhyme leaves the circle. The rhyme is repeated again and again until only one player remains in the circle. That person is IT. Here are two counting rhymes:**

One potato, two potato

Three potato, four

Five potato, six potato

Seven potato, more

> ### *or*

Bubble gum, bubble gum, in a dish

How many pieces do you wish?

(Player gives a number, like four)

One, two, three, four and

You are not IT

✳ **Grab a baseball bat or long stick. Gather around the bat. Put your hand on the very bottom. Quickly, all of the other players place their hands on top of yours. The person whose hand is at the very top is IT.**

Rules

Often players may know different versions of the same game. Go over all of the rules of a game before you start playing it. Agree on which version (or combination of versions) you want to play.

One of the best things about playing games is that you can make up your own rules. You can make up additional rules before the game starts, or, if the game is too easy or too hard, call a time-out and figure out what kind of new rules would make the game more fun. Then start the game over. Don't feel like you have to stick to the rules that are in this book. Simply make sure the rules are agreed on before playing, and play. See what happens.

How to End the Game

You can play until someone scores a specific number of points or until a goal is reached (like tagging everyone). Figure out before you start playing how many points you have to get to win, and agree on how much everything is worth. In some games you have to be more than one point ahead to win. If you don't want to play for a score, play for a specific amount of time (such as until dinnertime).

Being a Good Sport

The whole point of playing a game is to have fun, right? A lot of the games in this book have winners (and, therefore, losers). If you lose a game (or even 12 games in a row), so what? You're not a loser if you're having fun. Although, if someone's skills are much better than the rest of the players, how about making a rule to even the playing field? For instance, if you're playing Four Square and a much older kid has been dominating the fourth square the entire game, make a rule that anybody over the age of 12 has to play lefthanded.

So, what are you still reading this section for? Grab your friends, pick a game, get outside, play hard, play fair, and have fun!

Acorn Toss

Number of Players: **2 or more**

What You Need: **chalk, acorns**

Where to Play: **on the sidewalk**

The Point: **score points by accurately throwing acorns**

What You Do

1. Find a sidewalk square with lots of cracks on it, or use chalk to create your own.

2. With the chalk, connect the cracks in the sidewalk, making a bunch of different spaces. Number all of these spaces and make half of them negative numbers.

3. Decide what order you'll play in. Toss your acorn into the sidewalk square.

4. If your acorn lands on a positive space, add the number on that square to your score. If your acorn lands in a negative space, subtract that number of points from your score.

5. Leave your acorn where it is and let the next player go.

6. Players can try to knock one of the other player's acorns into a negative space. If that happens, that player has to subtract the number of points the space has written on it. If, however, the acorn is knocked into a different positive space, that acorn's player gets to add points.

7. The first player to score 20 points wins.

Other Ways to Play

✳ Use bottle caps or stones instead of acorns.

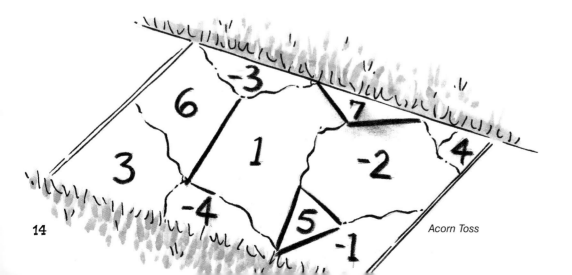

Acorn Toss

Amoeba Tag

Amoeba Tag

Number of Players: **6 or more**

What You Need**: clearly marked boundaries**

Where to Play: **in the yard or at the park**

The Point: **don't get swallowed by the Amoeba**

What You Do

1. Mark the boundaries. No one is allowed to leave the boundaries during the game. Pick the first player to be the Amoeba. The Amoeba tries to tag one of the other players.

2. If the Amoeba tags you, link arms with it. You're now a part of the Amoeba. Start chasing other players.

3. As other players are tagged, they must link arms with the Amoeba as well.

4. The Amoeba must stay connected. Only the players at the end of the chain (the ones with the free arm) can tag other players.

5. The last player tagged starts as the Amoeba in the next game.

Other Ways to Play

✳ If you have enough players, let the Amoeba break in half when it gets big enough. For instance, once the Amoeba is six players, it can split into two Amoebas that each have three players.

Balance Race

Number of Players: **2 or more**

What You Need: **start and finish line markers, stuff to balance (books, brooms, bats, plastic plates, sticks, or umbrellas)**

Where to Play: **in the yard**

The Point: **balance stuff while running a race**

What You Do

1. Mark the start and finish lines. Choose three things to balance on your hands and head.

2. Line up at the starting line, balancing your things.

3. On "go," run (or walk quickly) toward the finish line while balancing your items. If anything falls, you must stop and balance everything again before continuing.

4. The first player to reach the finish line wins.

Other Ways to Play

✳ Try a balancing competition with your feet. Lie on your back with your feet raised in the air. See who can balance the things on his or her feet the longest. (Obviously, you won't be able to race to the finish line with your feet up in the air.) To make this even more challenging, pretend to ride a bicycle while balancing the things on your feet.

Balancing Act

Number of Players: **2**

What You Need: **nothing**

Where to Play: **on the sidewalk**

The Point: **get to the end of a sidewalk crack and back without losing your balance**

What You Do

1. Find a section of the sidewalk that's covered with cracks.
2. Starting at opposite ends of a particularly intricate crack, you and the other player walk along the crack as if it were a tightrope. You must go all the way to the end of the crack and back without falling off.
3. If you lose your balance and step off the crack, return to the starting point.
4. The tricky part is when you meet and have to step around each other without losing your balance.
5. The first player to return to the starting point wins.

Other Ways to Play

- Bounce a ball on the crack as you move forward.
- Walk backward along the crack.

Ball between the Knees Race

Number of Players: **2 or more**

What You Need: **2 balls, large or small**

Where to Play: **in the pool**

The Point: **race with a ball between your knees**

What You Do

1. If you have more than two racers, divide into two teams. Decide what order your team will swim in.
2. Start at one end of the pool. Put the ball between your knees. On "go," swim to the other side of the pool. If you lose the ball, find it and start over from where you lost it.
3. Once you reach the other side of the pool, throw the ball to the next player on your team.
4. The first team to finish the race wins.

Other Ways to Play

- Put the ball between your feet and walk through the-shallow end of the pool for your race.
- Try this race with a beach ball between your knees.

Balloon Blanket Toss

Number of Players: **4 or more**

What You Need: **balloons, water, 2 blankets**

Where to Play: **in the yard**

The Point: **get wet**

What You Do

1. Fill the balloons with water. Divide into two teams and give each team a blanket.

2. Hold on to a piece of your blanket. Everyone on your team has to hold on to the blanket during the game.

3. Toss a water balloon back and forth to the other team with the blanket.

4. Keep track of how many times you can throw a balloon without breaking it.

5. When a water balloon breaks, get a new one and start counting again.

6. Whoever gets wet wins!

Other Ways to Play

❉ Toss more than one water balloon at a time.

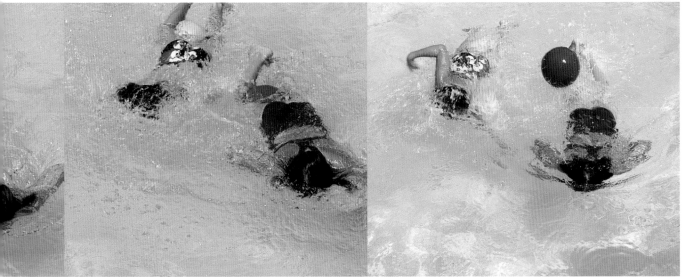

Ball between the Knees Race

Balls and Caps

Number of Players: **3 or more**

What You Need: **chalk, baseball cap and tennis ball for each player**

Where to Play: **against a wall**

The Point: **score the lowest number of points**

What You Do

1. Mark a throwing line parallel to the wall with the chalk. All of the players must stand behind this line to throw.

2. Place your cap upside down in front of the wall.

3. Toss or bounce your ball into another player's cap. Everyone plays at the same time.

4. If you miss the cap, you get a point. If your ball ends up in a cap, the player who owns that cap gets a point. (If you hit your own cap, you get a point.) Keep your own score, and be honest!

5. When you get your ball in a cap, run to it. All of the other players scatter. When you pick up the ball, yell "Freeze!"

6. All of the other players freeze. Toss your ball at one of them, aiming below the waist. The frozen players have to stay exactly where they are.

7. If you miss, you get a point. If the player is hit by the ball, that player gets a point.

8. At the end of the game (either after a set time or number of points), the player with the fewest points wins.

Baseless Baseball

Number of Players: **2 or more**

What You Need: **targets, tennis or racquet ball**

Where to Play: **in the yard or at the park**

The Point: **score runs by hitting targets**

What You Do

1. Choose four targets to aim at. You can gather your own targets, or you can use trees and whatever else is around. (Make sure they are safe targets to hit with a ball and that there aren't any innocent bystanders who could get hurt.)

2. Arrange the targets so some are more difficult to hit than others and award hits (singles, doubles, triples, and home runs) according to the level of difficulty in hitting each target.

3. Decide what order you'll play in.

4. Throw the ball at one of the targets. If you hit it, you get a ghost runner on that base. If you miss, you get an out.

5. Keep throwing at the targets until you have three outs. Then it's the next player's turn to bat. Each hit moves the ghost runners around the bases until they score.

6. Keep score and play as many innings as you like. The player with the most runs wins.

Other Ways to Play

❈ Use a Frisbee instead of a ball.

Baseless Baseball

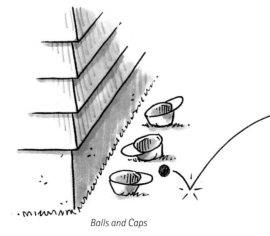

Balls and Caps

Basketball Games

Whether you're on a court or in your driveway, it's easy to re-create the excitement of a full-court game by playing one-on-one, two-on-two, or half the players versus the other half of the players. Or take your pick from any of the games that follow.

Around the World

Number of Players: **2 or more**
What You Need: **chalk, basketball**
Where to Play: **on a basketball court**
The Point: **make all the shots in order**

What You Do

1. Mark six or eight spots on the basketball court with the chalk. Number them. Decide what order you'll play in.

2. Try to hit each basket from numbers one to eight. Stand on the first spot and shoot. If you make the basket, move to the next spot and shoot again.

3. If you miss, you can let the next player go, or try the shot again. If you make it, you go on to the next shot. If you miss, you have to go back to the very first shot on your next turn. If you let the next player go instead of trying the shot again, you start from that spot on your next turn.

4. The first player to make all the shots wins.

Greedy

Number of Players: **2 or more**
What You Need: **basketball for each player**
Where to Play: **on a basketball court**
The Point: **make 10 baskets**

What You Do

1. All of the players stand the same distance from the basket with their basketballs.

2. On the count of three, everyone shoots at the basket. Rebound the first ball that comes your way.

3. Keep shooting as quickly as you can. You can shoot from anywhere on the court. When you make a basket, yell "One!" When you make the next one, yell "Two!" and so on.

4. Keep track of the number of baskets you score. The game ends when someone makes 10 baskets.

Other Ways to Play

❉ Have each basket count as two points, and create a three-point line for extra-long shots. The player who gets the most points wins.

Greedy

Horse

Number of Players: **2 or more**

What You Need: **basketball**

Where to Play: **on a basketball court**

The Point: **copy each other's shots**

What You Do

1. Decide what order you'll play in.
2. Take a shot from anywhere on the basketball court. (This is called the set-up shot). If the shot doesn't go in, the next player gets to choose a shot to attempt. If the shot goes in, all of the other players must copy this shot exactly.
3. Each player that misses the shot gets an "H."
4. After all of the players have taken a turn, shoot again from anywhere on the court. If the ball goes in, everyone else has to make that shot. If you miss your set-up shot, the next player gets to set up a shot. You don't get a letter for missing the set-up shot.
5. Every time you miss a shot (other than the set-up shot), you get another letter in the word "horse."
6. The first player to spell "horse" is out of the game. Keep playing until there's only one player left.

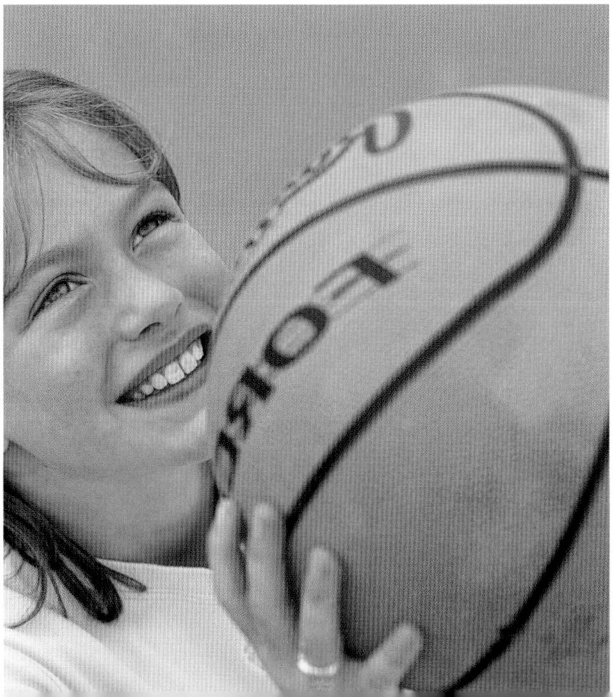

Rebound!

Number of Players: **2**

What You Need: **basketball**

Where to Play: **on a basketball court**

The Point: **score the most points**

What You Do

1. Decide who will go first. Stand behind the free throw line with the basketball. The other player stands beneath the net.
2. Shoot. If you make it in, the other player passes the ball back and you shoot again. Do this for as many times as you can, keeping track of your score.
3. If you miss, run as quickly as you can and grab the ball before it hits the ground. (The other player must get out of your way and not interfere at all.) Shoot again from where you were when you caught the ball. If you make it you get another point. Whether you hit or miss, give the ball to the other player.
4. The other player shoots while you stand under the net. Continue until you've both taken 10 turns.
5. The player with the most points wins.

Other Ways to Play

- If you're having trouble catching the ball before it hits the ground, try catching the ball after just one bounce, or two. Each player should have the same number of bounces to catch the ball, unless of course, you're playing against a basketball superstar, in which case, consider making it something like: "You catch it in the air, I get five bounces."

Basketball Court Tag

Number of Players: **3 or more**

What You Need: **nothing**

Where to Play: **on a basketball court**

The Point: **don't get tagged**

What You Do

1. Pick the first player to be IT. All of the other players stand on the painted lines of the basketball court.
2. You may not leave these lines for any reason. If you do, you automatically become IT.
3. IT chases all the other players, running along the lines trying to tag them. If you get tagged, you're IT.

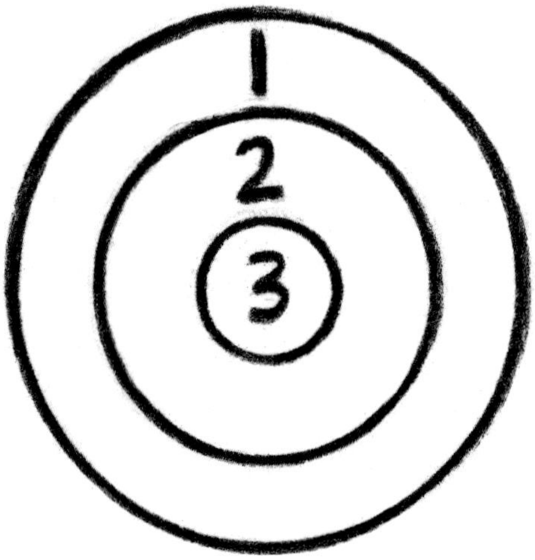

Beanbag Toss

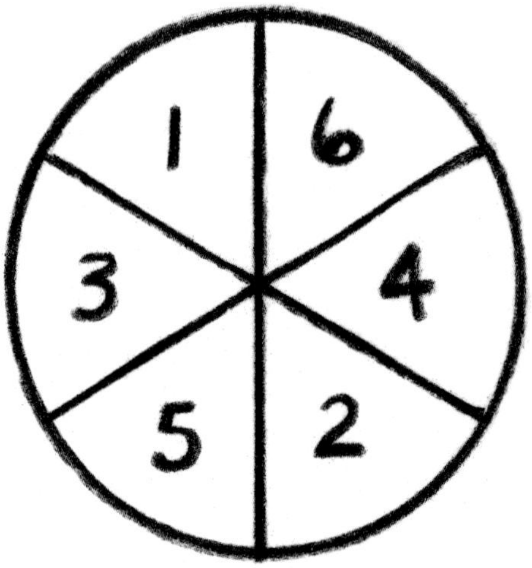

Beanbag Toss

Number of Players: **2 or more**

What You Need: **chalk, a beanbag for each player**

Where to Play: **on the sidewalk or on pavement**

The Point: **score the most points**

What You Do

1. Draw a target on the sidewalk with the chalk. It should be about 2 ½ feet across. Give each space in the target a different number. See the illustrations below for different target styles.
2. Mark a line at least 8 feet away from the target. This is the throwing line.
3. Decide what order you'll play in.
4. Take turns throwing the beanbags into the target. You get the number of points indicated in the area of the target your beanbag lands in. Keep track of your score.
5. The player with the most points at the end of the game wins.

How to Make a Beanbag

- You can make a beanbag out of an old sock and dry beans. Fill the toe of the sock with the dry beans and tie the top into a knot.

Other Ways to Play

- Use paper bags or buckets for the targets. Number them and take turns throwing your beanbag into each one in order. The first player to get his or her bean-bag in each target wins.

Behavior Modification

Number of Players: **3 or more**

What You Need: **nothing**

Where to Play: **anywhere**

The Point: **figure out what to do by listening to the cheers and boos**

What You Do

1. Pick the first player to be IT. IT goes away from all of the other players while they huddle.

2. While IT's out of earshot, all of the other players agree on a pose they want IT to adopt, such as sitting with legs crossed, lying down with one leg in the air, etc.

3. When the other players are ready, IT comes back and slowly begins moving ITs arms, legs, and body into different positions.

4. If IT's getting close to the agreed-on position, all of the other players clap and cheer. If IT's not, the players boo.

5. When IT finally gets the pose right, all of the other players cheer wildly.

6. Pick someone else to be IT.

Behind the Curtain

Number of Players: **4 or more**

What You Need: **rope, large sheet, boundary markers, balloons, water**

Where to Play: **in the yard or at a park**

The Point: **don't let the water balloon break**

What You Do

1. Get an adult to tie the rope between two trees so that it's a little bit above the tallest player's head. Drape the sheet over it. Mark equal boundaries on each side of the sheet. Fill the balloons with water.

2. Divide into two teams. Each team stands inside of the boundaries on one side of the sheet with half of the water balloons.

3. Toss two balloons back and forth over the sheet. If a balloon is dropped or burst, the team on the side that the balloon broke gets a penalty point. Toss in a new water balloon.

4. After all the water balloons are gone, the team with the least number of points wins.

Other Ways to Play

❊ If you don't want to play with water balloons, use softballs instead.

❊ To make things more challenging, add two more balloons each time one is broken.

❊ See how many balloons you can have going back and forth at a time.

Beanbag Toss Variation

Bicycle Unrace

Number of Players: **2 or more**

What You Need: **chalk, a bike for each racer**

Where to Play: **on the sidewalk**

The Point: **cross the finish line last**

What You Do

1. Mark the start and finish lines with the chalk.

2. Line up behind the start line with your bikes. On "go," start pedaling as slowly as you possibly can toward the finish line.

3. You may not touch the ground with your feet and you have to keep going forward.

4. The last player to cross the finish line wins.

Blind Man's Buff

Number of Players: **3 or more**

What You Need: **boundary markers, blindfold**

Where to Play: **in the yard**

The Point: **don't get tagged**

What You Do

1. Mark the boundaries. Blindfold the first player who will be IT.

2. While IT spins around five times, all of the other players run around to find a good hiding spot within the boundaries.

3. After the last spin, IT yells "Stop," and everybody freezes.

4. IT searches for the other players by calling, "Blind Man's…" You must yell "Buff" in response every time. IT tries to find you by following your voice.

5. You cannot move your feet, but you can move the rest of your body to avoid being tagged.

6. The first player tagged is IT for the next game.

Bicycle Unrace

British Bulldog

Number of Players: **4 to 10**

What You Need: **nothing**

Where to Play: **in the yard or at the park**

The Point: **be the last one tagged**

What You Do

1. Pick the first player to be IT. All the other players line up, facing IT.

2. On "go," everyone runs past IT while IT tries to tag them.

3. If you get tagged, help catch the nontagged players.

4. The last player to get tagged wins and is IT in the next round.

Brooklyn Bridge

Number of Players: **6 or more**

What You Need: **a kick ball**

Where to Play: **on pavement**

The Point: **roll the ball between your opponent's legs**

What You Do

1. Divide into two teams and line up facing each other. The teams should be about 15 feet apart. Spread your legs wide enough for the ball to be able to roll between them.

2. Each team takes turns trying to roll the ball between the legs of one of the players on the opposite team. No one may move or try to block the ball in any way when it is rolled at them.

3. If the ball passes between your legs, the other team either scores a point or you are out, depending on how you want to play. (Don't play elimination unless you have really big teams.)

4. The game is over when everybody but one person has been eliminated or when an agreed-on score has been reached.

Bubble Race

Bubble Race

Number of Players: **2 or more**

What You Need: **start and finish line markers, bubbles and wand for each player**

Where to Play: **in the yard**

The Point: **get your bubble across the finish line first**

What You Do

1. Mark a start and finish line 15 to 20 feet apart.

2. Line up behind the starting line.

3. On "go," blow a single bubble, catch it on your wand, and start moving toward the finish line.

4. If your bubble pops, stop moving and blow another bubble. Catch it on your wand, then continue toward the finish line.

5. The first player who crosses the finish line wins.

Super Sudsy Bubble Solution

Mix 1 cup of dishwashing liquid (the kind you use to wash dishes by hand) with 3 cups of water. Add ½ cup of corn syrup. Mix it together.

Super Easy Bubble Blower

Make a loop at one end of a piece of wire. Use this as your bubble blower.

Other Ways to Play

❊ After blowing a bubble, don't catch it on your wand. Instead, try to fan, blow, or wave the bubble over the finish line.

Bucket Ball

Number of Players: **4 or more**

What You Need: **large bucket, chalk, small rubber ball, timer (optional)**

Where to Play: **on the sidewalk**

The Point: **score the most points for your team**

What You Do

1. Place the bucket on the ground and draw a line around it with the chalk. No one can cross this line.

2. Mark a start line a good distance from the bucket with the chalk. You can make this a circle that goes all the way around the other chalk line, or a straight line. You will be bouncing the ball into the bucket, so give yourself plenty of room. (You can always move the line if the game is too hard or too easy.)

3. Divide into two teams and decide how long you're going to play the game. Set a timer if you want.

4. Stand behind the starting line and throw the ball, trying to make it bounce once and enter the bucket. If the ball goes in, your team gets a point and the other team gets a turn.

5. If the ball doesn't go in, all of the players run to catch it. If you get the ball, you can't move, but you can pass it to one of your teammates.

6. Once the ball is across the starting line, it can be shot again.

7. You can intercept passes or try to steal the ball. Once the other team has gotten the ball over the starting line, though, you may not interfere.

8. The game continues until the time limit is up. The team with the most points wins.

Bungle Bungle

Number of Players: **3 or more**

What You Need: **boundary markers, a half-filled water balloon and 3-foot-long piece of string for each player**

Where to Play: **in the yard or at a park**

The Point: **break everybody's water balloon**

What You Do

1. Mark a square playing area, large enough for all the players to run around easily inside it.

2. Use the 3-foot-long pieces of string to tie a water balloon to each player's wrist.

3. Run around in the playing area, swinging your balloon. Try to burst all of the other players' balloons with yours. Don't let your balloon break.

4. If your balloon breaks, stand outside the playing area until the game is finished.

5. The last player with a balloon wins.

Other Ways to Play

❈ Tie a balloon to each wrist and stay in the game until both of your balloons are busted.

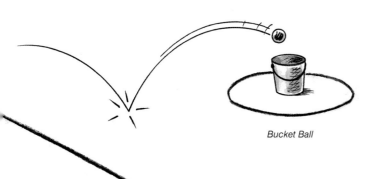

Bucket Ball

Buried Treasure

Number of Players: **2 or more**

What You Need: **treasure, plastic bag (optional), pencil, paper**

Where to Play: **in the yard or at the beach**

The Point: **find the buried treasure**

What You Do

1. Decide who will hide the treasure first.

2. Bury the treasure somewhere. The treasure can be anything: an old soda bottle, chocolate chip cookies, or even your big brother's stinky gym socks. If the treasure needs a little extra protection from whatever it's being buried in (like chocolate chip cookies would), put it in a plastic bag first.

3. After you've buried the treasure, draw a map. The map could say something like "Walk 10 steps past the guy sleeping on the red towel, face the ocean, and turn right," or it could just be a series of landmarks with the location of the buried treasure marked with an X.

4. Give the other players the map so that they can look for the treasure.

5. When the treasure is found, pick another player to bury something.

Capture the Flag

Number of Players: **6 or more**

What You Need: **flags (a brightly colored shirt or piece of fabric works well)**

Where to Play: **In a large backyard or at a park**

The Point: **capture the other team's flag**

What You Do

1. Divide the playing area down the middle and split into two teams. Each team gets one side of the playing area and picks a spot for the jail. You must show the other team where your jail is.

2. Put your flag somewhere on your side. It must be visible to the other team and easy to get at, but you don't have to tell them where it is. (That means you can't hide it at the top of the highest tree, stuffed inside a squirrel's nest.) You may not move the flag to a different spot during the game.

3. When the game begins, sneak onto the other team's territory and try to find the flag. If you see the flag, grab it and run back to your side. Watch out for the other team. They will chase you and try to tag you.

4. If you get tagged in the other team's court, you have to go to the jail. You can tag a member of the opposite team only when he or she is on your side of the playing area. If you've got the flag when you get tagged, it is returned to its original position.

Buried Treasure

5. You can rescue your teammates from the jail by tagging them.

6. Once you snatch the other team's flag and get it back to your side without getting tagged, the game is over.

Other Ways to Play

- Give each team more than one flag. You have to collect them all to win. You can recapture captured flags.
- If you'd like a more challenging game, teams can "hide" their flags. (The flags must be showing enough to be seen from 10 feet away.)
- Tuck the flag into one player's shirt from each team, hanging down his or her back.
- Use water balloons to tag the other players.

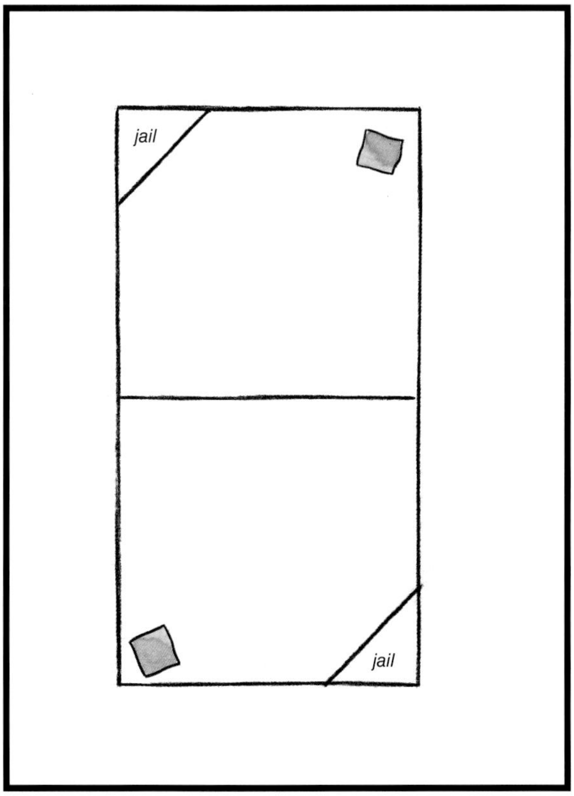

Capture the Flag

Cat and Mouse

Number of Players: **8 or more**

What You Need: **nothing**

Where to Play: **in the yard**

The Point: **don't let the Cat eat the Mouse**

What You Do

1. Choose the first player to be the Cat, and another to be the Mouse.
2. All of the other players hold hands and form a circle around the Mouse, with the Cat on the outside.
3. The Cat tries to break into the circle and eat the Mouse. The players that make up the circle squish together to keep the Cat out.
4. If the Cat gets into the circle, the Mouse scurries out of the circle and runs around it. The Cat follows and chases the Mouse.
5. If the Mouse makes it all the way around the circle and back to where he or she broke out, the Mouse goes back into the circle and the game keeps going. If the Mouse is caught, he or she has to lie on the ground and play dead while the Cat pretends to eat it.
6. Choose a new Cat and Mouse and keep on playing.

Other Ways to Play

- Set a limit on how much time the Cat has to catch the Mouse.
- Instead of squishing together, hold your arms up to let the Cat through and down to keep the Cat out.

Catch a Sponge

Number of Players: **4 or more**

What You Need: **something to mark the throwing lines, water-filled bucket, lots of sponges, plastic bowl for each team**

Where to Play: **in the yard**

The Point: **get soaking wet**

What You Do

1. Mark the throwing lines about 7 feet apart. Divide into two teams and line up facing each other behind the throwing lines. Place the bucket of water an equal distance from both teams and fill it with the sponges.

2. Pick the first player to be your team's catcher. The catcher gets one of the plastic bowls and stands behind the other team's throwing line.

3. At "go," everyone runs to the bucket and grabs a sponge. You can pick up only one sponge at a time. Go back to the throwing line.

4. Throw the sponge into your catcher's bowl. The catcher has to stand in one place but can move the bowl to catch the sponges.

5. You can throw wet sponges at the other team to distract them.

6. Collect the uncaught sponges on your side and return them to the bucket when you go back to get a new sponge.

7. When you run out of sponges, the team that has caught the most sponges wins.

Other Ways to Play

✳ Forget the plastic bowls—catch the sponges with your bare hands!

✳ Switch out the catcher so that everybody has a chance to get really wet.

✳ Play regular catch with the sponges.

Chair Carry

Number of Players: **6 or more**

What You Need: **start and finish line markers**

Where to Play: **in the yard**

The Point: **carry every member of your team over the finish line**

What You Do

1. Mark the start and finish lines a good distance apart. Divide into teams of three. It's helpful if all the members of a team are about the same size.

2. Line up in front of the start line and decide which member of your team will be the first one carried, and which two players will be the first ones carrying.

3. The two players who will be carrying make their hands into a chair. To do this, grab your right wrist with your left hand. The other player does the same. Then take hold of each other's left wrists with your right hands. Your arms will form a square that the player you're carrying can sit on. (If you're being carried, wrap your arms around the shoulders of the people carrying you.)

4. On "go," race to the finish line. Once across, switch places so that another player is carried on the chair. Race back to the starting line. Then switch players again so that everyone has a chance to be carried, and run back to the finish line.

5. The first team to make it across the finish line is the winner.

Other Ways to Play

❄ Play in the shallow end of a swimming pool, where the teams can walk in the water.

Chimp Race

Number of Players: **2 or more**

What You Need: **start and finish line markers**

Where to Play: **in the yard**

The Point: **make it across the finish line first**

What You Do

1. Mark the start and finish lines. Line up behind the starting line.

2. Bend down and hold onto your ankles with your hands.

3. On "go," race toward the finish line. You must keep hold of your ankles the entire time.

4. The first player to cross the finish line wins.

Chair Carry

Chimp Race

Clothespins

Number of Players: **5 or more**

What You Need: **lots of clothespins**

Where to Play: **in the yard or at the park**

The Point: **keep your clothespins on**

What You Do

1. Each player attaches three clothespins to the sleeve or bottom of his or her T-shirt. (You can use a different number of clothespins if you like, but make sure each player starts with the same number of clothespins.)

2. When the game begins, try to steal the clothespins off other players' shirts. You can move away to keep someone from stealing your clothespins, but you cannot push anybody's hand away or cover your clothespins.

3. You can take only one clothespin from another player at a time. After you've grabbed a clothespin, count out loud to three while you attach it to your shirt. During this time, nobody can steal any of your clothespins.

4. At the end of the game, the person with the most clothespins wins.

Cold Potato

Number of Players: **3 or more**

What You Need: **balloons, safety pin, water**

Where to Play: **anywhere**

The Point: **don't get stuck with an empty balloon**

What You Do

1. Poke a hole in a balloon with the safety pin. Fill it with water.

2. Stand in a circle and pass the balloon around.

3. Whoever is holding the balloon when it runs out of water loses. (But if it's a hot day, is it really losing?)

Cold Potato

Contrary Simon Says

Contrary Simon Says

Number of Players: **3 or more**
What You Need: **nothing**
Where to Play: **anywhere**
The Point: **don't do what Simon says**

What You Do

1. Pick the first player to be Simon. All of the other players line up, facing Simon.

2. Simon calls out actions for the players to perform. If Simon says "Simon says" first, then do the opposite of whatever you are told to do. For instance, if Simon says, "Simon says hop up and down on your right foot," you should hop up and down on your left foot.

3. If Simon doesn't say "Simon says" before calling out an action, don't do anything.

4. Simon watches the rest of the players very carefully. If someone does what Simon says, or moves when Simon hasn't said "Simon says," that player is out.

5. When only one player besides Simon remains, that player gets to be the new Simon.

Other Ways to Play

✲ If Simon doesn't say "Simon says," you have to do that exact action.

Crab Soccer

Crab Soccer

Number of Players: **6 or more**

What You Need: **boundary and goal markers, a soccer ball**

Where to Play: **in the yard or at a park**

The Point: **score the most points**

What You Do

1. Mark the boundaries of the playing area and make two goals. Divide into two teams.

2. Teams lie on their backs and then push themselves off the ground with their hands and feet. This is the crab position.

3. You must remain in this position during play. You can't touch the ball with your hands. You have to kick it.

4. Each team tries to dribble, pass, or kick the ball into the opponent's goal. Teams can have goalies if they want, but they aren't required.

5. When a team scores a point, the ball goes to the other team. If the ball goes out of bounds, the last player to touch it has to go get it and then give it to the other team.

6. The team that scores the most points wins.

Dizzy Izzy

Cross Tag

Number of Players: **3 or more**

What You Need: **nothing**

Where to Play: **in the yard or at the park**

The Point: **use teamwork to confuse IT and be the last one tagged**

What You Do

1. Pick the first player to be IT.

2. IT calls out the name of one of the players. All of the players start running, but IT may chase only the player that IT named.

3. When any other player passes between IT and the player that IT is chasing, IT has to start chasing the new player.

4. The other players should use teamwork to keep IT from tagging anyone.

5. When IT tags the player IT was chasing, that player becomes the new IT and the game begins again.

Dizzy Izzy

Number of Players: **2 or more**

What You Need: **start and finish line markers, a baseball bat for each player**

Where to Play: **in the yard or at a park**

The Point: **get dizzy and run a race**

What You Do

1. Mark the start and finish lines. Divide into teams and line up behind the start line.

2. On "go," the first racer from each team stands the baseball bat up on one end, leans over, and puts his or her forehead on that bat. Spin around five times, keeping your head on the bat and the bat on the ground. (Make players spin around more times if the game is too easy, and fewer times if they're turning green.)

3. After you've spun around five times, drop the bat and run toward the finish line. Then turn around and run back.

4. When you cross the start line, tag the next racer from your team.

5. The first team to have all its members get back across the start line wins.

Other Ways to Play

✱ Blindfold the players before they spin.

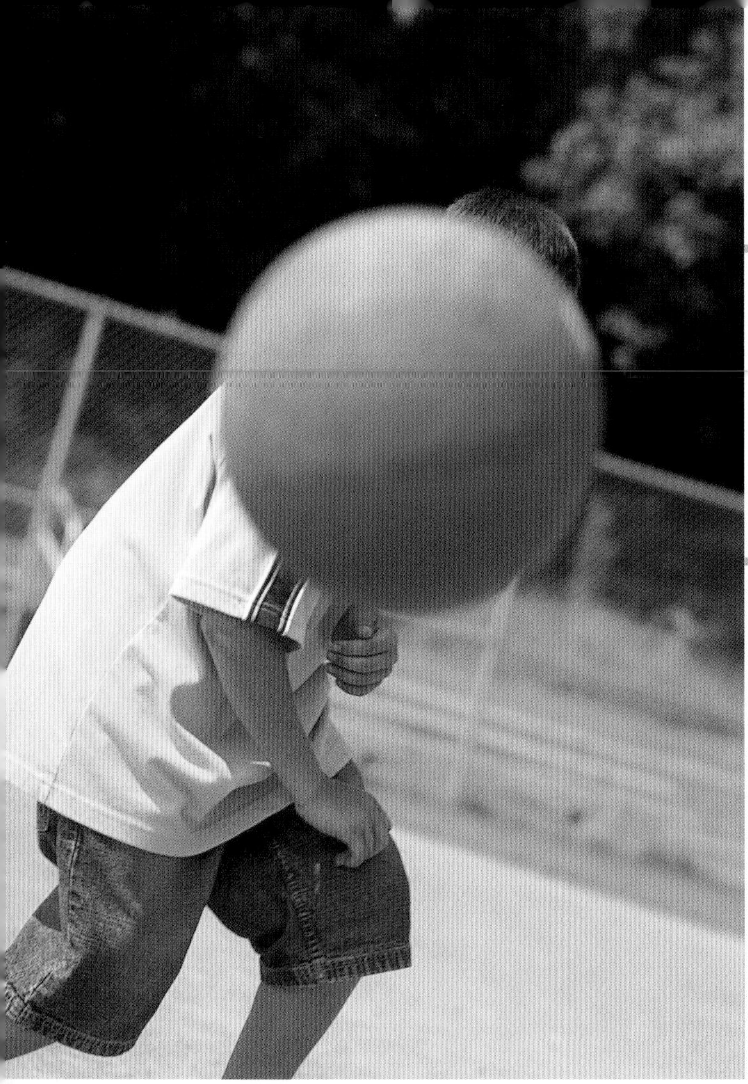

Dodge Ball Games

Dodge ball is a great game, with lots of different ways to play. Pick the version that sounds like the most fun to you.

Dodge Ball

Number of Players: **5 or more**
What You Need: **chalk, dodge ball**
Where to Play: **at the park or on pavement**
The Point: **don't get hit by the ball**

What You Do

1. Mark a large circle and pick the first player to be IT.
2. IT stands inside the circle. All of the other players stand outside of it.
3. Throw the ball back and forth through the circle, trying to tag IT below the waist with the ball. If you hit IT above the waist, your throw doesn't count.
4. If you hit IT, you get to go in the middle and dodge. If IT catches the ball, IT has to give it back.

Other Ways to Play

- If IT catches the ball you threw, you're out.

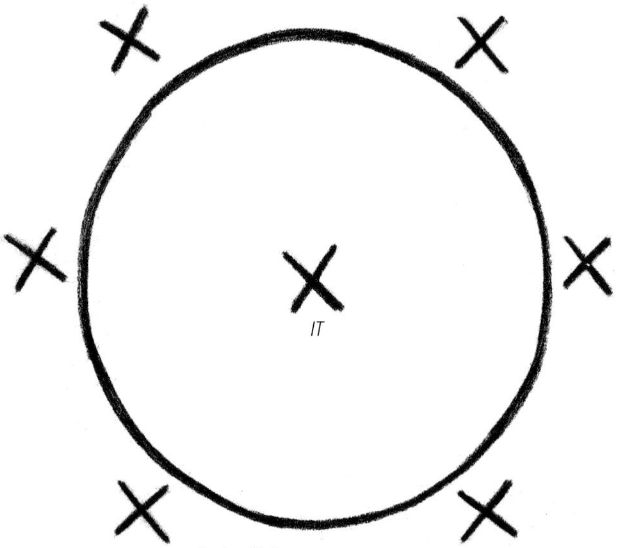

Dodge Ball

Dodge Ball Reverse

Number of Players: **5 or more**

What You Need: **dodge ball**

Where to Play: **at the park or on pavement**

The Point: **don't get any points**

What You Do

1. Pick the first player to be IT.

2. IT stands in the middle of the playing area with the ball. All of the other players pick a color. They stand in two lines in front of and behind IT.

3. IT calls out a color. If IT calls your color, you must run to the other line before IT throws the ball (aiming below the waist) and tags you.

4. If you get hit, you get one point and replace IT in the middle. If IT misses, IT stays in the middle.

5. The game continues until only one player has no score. That player wins.

Other Ways to Play

❋ Instead of using colors, use numbers, letters, your favorite superheroes, or any other category you can think of to play.

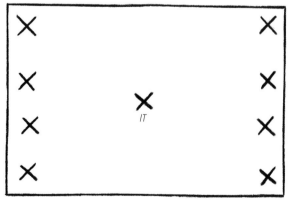

Dodge Ball Reverse

Dodge War

Number of Players: **5 or more**

What You Need: **boundary markers, dodge ball**

Where to Play: **at the park or on pavement**

The Point: **score the most points**

What You Do

1. Mark a large, rectangular playing area and divide into two teams. Pick one player to be the first referee.

2. Number off, so that each member of your team has a number. There will be a player on the other team that has the same number.

3. Line up with your team behind one side of the rectangle. The other team lines up on the opposite side. Place the ball in the middle of the rectangle.

4. The referee calls out a number. If it's your number, you and the member of the other team that has that number run into the playing area, trying to pick up the ball first.

5. When you get the ball, you must stand still and count out loud to 10. The other player can move around but has to stay within the rectangle.

6. Throw the ball at the other player, aiming below the waist. If you hit the other player, your team scores a point. If you don't, return the ball to the middle of the rectangle and go back to your side.

7. The first team to score 21 points wins.

Freeze Dodge Ball

Number of Players: **5 or more**

What You Need: **boundary markers, dodge ball**

Where to Play: **at the park or on pavement**

The Point: **don't get hit by the ball**

What You Do

1. Mark a large circle and divide into two teams.
2. Play like regular dodge ball, except that the first time you get hit with the ball, your left leg freezes.
3. The second time you get hit by the ball, your right leg freezes.
4. The third time you get hit by the ball, your left arm freezes.
5. The fourth time you get hit by the ball, your right arm freezes. Since you can no longer move, the next time you get hit by the ball, you're out.
6. The team that still has players in the game at the end wins.

Team Dodge Ball

Number of Players: **5 or more**

What You Need: **boundary markers, dodge ball**

Where to Play: **at the park or on pavement**

The Point: **get the other team out**

What You Do

1. Mark a large rectangle for the playing area. Divide it down the middle and pick two teams. Each team stands in one-half of the playing area.
2. Team members take turns running up to the dividing line and throwing the ball at one of the other team's players, aiming below the waist. If you get hit with a ball below the waist, you're out. The ball must hit the other player before it touches the ground to count as an out.
3. If the player you're throwing the ball at catches it, you're out.
4. The team that still has players at the end of the game wins.

Other Ways to Play

* If you get out, join the team on the other side. The first team with all the players wins.

Everybody's It

Number of Players: **5 or more**

What You Need: **nothing**

Where to Play: **in the yard or at the park**

The Point: **tag everybody**

What You Do

1. In this game, everybody's IT. To start the game, start chasing each other.

2. If you get tagged, you have to freeze right where you are. You may unfreeze an arm to tag a player who runs too close to you, but you cannot move your feet.

3. If you and somebody else both tag each other at the same time, you're both frozen.

4. The game continues until there's only one player left unfrozen.

Other Ways to Play

❊ To make the game last forever (or at least until everybody's tired), you can tag frozen players to unfreeze them, or frozen players become unfrozen when they tag someone else.

Five Dollars

Number of Players: **3 or more**

What You Need: **small rubber ball and plastic bat or baseball, bat, and mitts**

Where to Play: **in the park or ball field**

The Point: **earn "money" catching the ball**

What You Do

1. Pick the first player to be the batter. All of the other players stand in the field.

2. The batter hits the ball to the players.

3. The players try to catch the ball in order to earn "money." (Sorry, no real money is exchanged.)

4. If you catch the ball in the air, you earn one dollar. If you pick it up after one bounce, you get 75 cents. If you pick it up after two bounces, you get 50 cents. If you catch a rolling ball, you get 25 cents.

5. As soon as you earn five dollars, you get to bat. The other players get to keep the money they've earned so far.

Other Ways to Play

❊ Assign points instead of money. Give different amounts of points for different actions. You can even make up your own kinds of fielding actions, such as catching between your legs, catching with your nondominant hand, or even catching with your baseball cap.

❊ When you change batters, start everyone over at zero.

Five Dollars

Fivestones

Number of Players: **2 or more**
What You Need: **5 stones**
Where to Play: **on the sidewalk**
The Point: **catch as many of the stones as possible**

What You Do

1. To figure out who will start the game, each player throws five stones in the air and tries to catch as many as possible on the back of that same hand. Throw the stones into the air again with the back of your hand and catch as many as you can in your palm. The player who has caught the most stones goes first.

2. Throw five stones into the air with one hand. Try to catch them on the back of that same hand before they hit the ground.

3. If you don't catch any of the stones on the back of your hand, it's the next player's turn. If you catch some of the stones on the back of your hand, throw them into the air again, and catch them in the palm of that hand.

4. Keep one of the stones in the hand you are throwing with. Toss all of the other stones on the sidewalk in front of you.

5. Throw the stone in your hand into the air. Pick up one of the stones on the ground with that same hand, and then catch the stone you threw. If you make it, go again until all the stones have been picked up. You must use the same hand for everything.

6. Once you've picked up all of the stones, throw four of them down again. Throw the one remaining stone into the air, pick up two of the other stones, and catch the one you threw. Next time, pick up the last two stones.

7. On the next round, pick up three of the stones at once, and on the final round, pick up all of the stones at one time.

8. If at any point you don't pick up all the stones in your turn, or don't catch the stone before it falls, the next player gets to go.

9. The first player to make it all the way through the rounds wins.

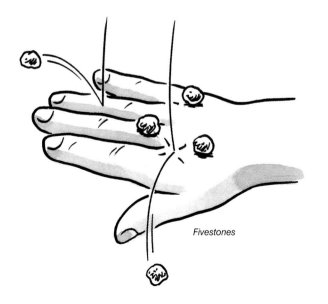

Fivestones

Flashlight Tag

Number of Players: **4 or more**
What You Need: **flashlight for every player**
Where to Play: **in the yard at night**
The Point: **find your partner using flashlight signals**

What You Do

1. Pair off so that every player has a partner. Sneak off with your partner and figure out what your flashlight signal will be (one short and one long flash, three short flashes, and so on).

2. After everybody's figured out the flashlight signals, partners go to opposite ends of the yard. All of the players count out loud to 50.

3. After you've counted to 50, start flashing your signal at the other end of the yard where your partner is. Try to find each other.

4. The first pair to find each other wins.

Flutter Ball

Number of Players: **2 or more**
What You Need: **coins, tape, foam ball, ping pong ball**
Where to Play: **in the yard**
The Point: **play with some seriously misbehaving balls**

How to Play

1. Tape a coin to the foam ball. Play catch with it.

2. Tape another coin to the foam ball and play volley-ball. If you don't have a net, just bounce the ball to the other players and see how long you can keep it in the air.

3. Tape a coin to the ping pong ball and play catch with it. Keep playing until you get dizzy.

Follow the Leader

Number of Players: **2 or more**
What You Need: **nothing**
Where to Play: **in the yard or at the park**
The Point: **imitate the person in front of you**

What You Do

1. Pick the first player to be the Leader. All of the other players line up behind the Leader.

2. The Leader starts walking, jumping, skipping, or whatever. All of the other players must do the same thing. For instance, if the Leader stops to touch a telephone pole, all of the other players must touch the telephone pole in the exact same way.

3. After a set time, the Leader goes to the back of the line. The player in front is the new Leader.

Four Square

Number of Players: **4 or more**
What You Need: **chalk, bouncy ball**
Where to Play: **on pavement**
The Point: **get to the fourth square**

What You Do

1. Draw a large square about 2 to 3 yards on each side with the chalk. Divide that square into four smaller squares all the same size. Write the numbers one through four in the squares.

2. Decide what order you'll play in. The first four players each stand in one of the squares. The other players line up behind the first square.

3. The player in the fourth square begins the game. Bounce the ball inside your square then bat it into one of the other squares. The ball has to reach the other square in only one bounce or else you're out.

4. If the ball comes to your square, bounce it into someone else's square. You do not have to bounce it in your own square first (that only happens when you serve).

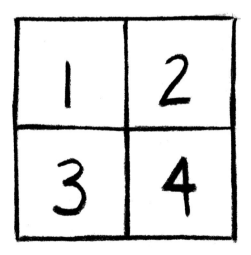

Four Square

42

5. If you miss the ball or bounce it out of bounds, you're out. Leave your square and go stand behind the other players waiting their turn to play.

6. The players that were standing in squares with lower numbers than yours all move up one square. A new player moves into the first square. For example, if you were on the third square and got out, the player in the second square would take your square, the player in the first square would take the second square, and the first player in line would move into the first square.

7. The player in the fourth square always serves.

Other Ways to Play

✢ Let the server call out special ways to play. When you make one of these calls, all of the other players must do the appropriate action immediately. The last person to do the right action is out.

Bus stop: Step on the outer corner of your square.

Fire alarm: Jump out of your square.

Mailbox: Step in the middle where the two lines meet.

Big tomato: Do a mailbox and then a fire alarm.

Around the world: When players bounce the ball, they must also call out a color—or state, animal, pizza topping, or whatever category the server has called. You can't repeat things other players have said.

Normal: Play goes back to normal.

Four Square

Fox and Geese

Number of Players: **3 or more**

What You Need: **chalk**

Where to Play: **on pavement**

The Point: **don't get caught by the Fox**

What You Do

1. Draw a path on the pavement with the chalk. Make sure it's wide enough everywhere for your feet to fit inside it. Draw a large square or circle in the middle of the track to be the holding pen.

2. Pick the first player to be the Fox. All of the other players are Geese.

3. The Fox chases the Geese around the track. If you step out of the track you have to go to the holding pen in the middle.

4. When the Fox catches a Goose, the Goose goes in the holding pen. Other Geese can release the caught Goose, but they have to sneak past the Fox and into the holding pen to tag the Goose.

5. The last player caught is the next Fox.

Other Ways to Play

❊ This is a great game to play in the winter if you can find a large spot of undisturbed snow. Make a track through the snow by walking in single file. Create the holding pen by trampling down snow in the middle of the course. Let each player make one shortcut between parts of the path.

Fox and Geese

Freeze Tag

Number of Players: **5 or more**

What You Need: **boundary markers**

Where to Play: **in the yard or at the park**

The Point: **don't get frozen**

What You Do

1. Mark the boundaries and pick the first player to be IT.

2. To begin the game, everyone starts running around. IT tries to tag all of the players. If you get tagged, freeze. You cannot move at all.

3. Other players can tag frozen players. Once tagged, frozen players unfreeze and can run around again. IT tries to keep all the players frozen.

4. The last person to be frozen gets to be IT in the next round.

Other Ways to Play

❊ Instead of just tagging frozen players, crawl between their legs to unfreeze them.

Frisbee Football

Frisbee Football

Number of Players: **4 or more**
What You Need: **boundary markers, Frisbee**
Where to Play: **a large grassy area**
The Point: **score the most goals**

What You Do

1. Mark the boundaries and goal lines. Divide into two teams.

2. Decide which team will go first and who the quarterback for each team will be.

3. Give the quarterback the Frisbee and begin the game. You can't run with the Frisbee, you have to pass it back and forth to your teammates to move toward your opponent's goal line.

4. The defending team tries to intercept the Frisbee. You can guard the other players by waving your arms, jumping up and down, screaming, or doing impressions of your math teacher, but you may not touch the other players.

5. When you catch the Frisbee, mark the spot. If the Frisbee is fumbled, the game will start over at that spot.

6. When the Frisbee is intercepted, it goes to the other team. Keep playing from wherever you are when the Frisbee is intercepted.

7. When a team catches the Frisbee in their opponent's goal, they get seven points.

8. After one team scores a touchdown, the other team gets the Frisbee.

9. The team that scores the most points wins.

Frisbee Golf

Number of Players: **2 to 7**
What You Need: **targets, Frisbee, paper, pencil**
Where to Play: **at the park**
The Point: **hit each target in the fewest number of tries**

What You Do

1. Pick targets and decide in what order you'll hit them.

2. Decide what order you'll play in. All of the players line up in front of the first target.

3. Throw the Frisbee at the first target. If you hit it, give yourself one point. If you miss, run to where the Frisbee landed, pick it up, and throw it at the target again. Keep doing this until you hit the target. You get one point for each try. Write down the number of tries it took you to hit the target. Then give the Frisbee to the next player.

4. When every player has hit the first target, all of the players move on to the second target. Continue to play until all of the players have hit all the targets, keeping score with the paper and pencil.

5. Add up your points. The player with the fewest points wins.

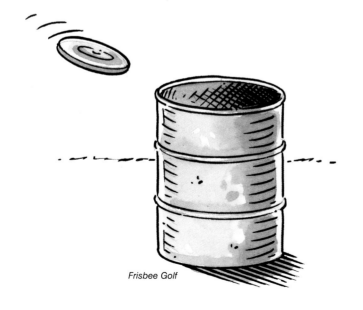

Frisbee Golf

German

Number of Players: **4 to 8**
What You Need: **chalk, small rubber ball**
Where to Play: **on pavement against a wall**
The Point: **score the most runs**

What You Do

1. Draw a court on the pavement with the chalk. Divide the court into four parts: the batter's box and sections one, two, and three. See the illustration on page 47.

2. Divide into two teams. Decide which team will be at bat first.

3. The first player from the team at bat is the batter. The batter stands in the batter's box, and two or three players from the other team stand in spaces one through three.

4. The batter bats by throwing the ball against the wall. It must bounce once in the batter's box.

5. The other players on the court try to catch the ball. If the ball bounces out of bounds, it's a foul, and the batter tries again.

6. If the ball is caught in square one, the batter has a single. If it's caught in square two, it's a double. If it's caught in square three, it's a triple. If the ball goes beyond square three, it's a home run.

7. If the player trying to catch the ball just manages to knock it out of bounds, the batter scores the same as if the ball were caught in that square.

8. Each batter on the team gets to bat twice.

9. The next batter's score can be added to the previous batter's score if the players are on the same team. After each player has batted, the teams switch places. None of the hits from this inning carry over.

10. Play five innings. The team with the most runs at the end of the game wins.

Other Ways to Play

� If you've got only two players, play for points instead of runs. Section one is worth one point, two is two points, three is three points, and a home run is four points. Each player bats five times before switching places. The player with the high score at the end of the game wins.

✺ If there are only three players, one stands between box one and two and the other stands between box two and three while the last player bats.

Germs and Doctors

Number of Players: **10 or more**
What You Need: **nothing**
Where to Play: **in the yard or at the park**
The Point: **don't get sick**

What You Do

1. Pick the first players to be Germs. There should be one Germ for every five players. Pick the first players to be Doctors. There should be one Doctor for every 10 players.

2. The Germs run around, trying to infect everybody they can by tagging them. If you get infected, fall to the ground and yell "Doctor! Doctor!" If one of the Doctors tags you, you're cured and can run around again.

3. Germs can infect Doctors too. If a Doctor gets tagged, another Doctor has to come and cure him or her.

4. If all the Doctors get infected, nobody can be cured anymore. At this point, pick new Germs and Doctors.

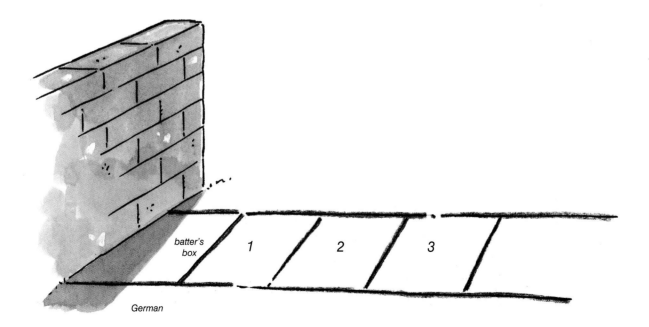

batter's box   1   2   3

German

Goal Kickers

Number of Players: **6 or more**
What You Need: **chalk, soccer ball**
Where to Play: **on pavement**
The Point: **score the most points**

What You Do

1. Mark a large, rectangular field with the chalk. (For a game with eight players, 20 by 40 feet is a good size.) Divide it in half.

2. Split into two teams. Each team stands in one-half of the rectangle. Players are not allowed to cross the dividing line.

3. Play begins with a tip-off. One player from each team stands on either side of the dividing line, facing each other. Another player (teams take turns choosing one) tosses the ball up between the two players. They jump up and try to bat the ball to their team. (This is the only time the players can touch the ball with their hands.)

4. Teams try to kick the ball past the other team and across the line at the back of the field to score a point. You may not touch the ball with your hands, but you can use any other body part possible. If you touch the ball with your hands, the other team gets it.

5. If a point is scored or the ball goes out of bounds, have another tip-off.

6. The first team to score 21 points wins.

Gold Glove

Number of Players: **2 or more**
What You Need: **baseball, 2 baseball mitts**
Where to Play: **in a grassy area**
The Point: **play catch**

What You Do

1. Line up about 30 feet away from your partner.

2. Play catch, counting each time you and your partner catch the ball. If you drop the ball, start over at zero.

Other Ways to Play

❋ Use any kind of ball to play. It doesn't even have to be a ball—try using a frisbee or counting badminton hits. If you like football, count the number of passes/receptions a receiver can complete in a row.

❋ Start the game by standing very close to your partner. Each time you make a successful catch, take a step back.

❋ Play against a wall. Bounce the ball off the wall, then catch it.

Golf Ball Billiards

Number of Players: **2 or more**

What You Need: **chalk, 10 golf balls, sticks**

Where to Play: **on the sidewalk**

The Point: **knock as many balls as you can out of the circle**

What You Do

1. Draw a circle on the pavement with the chalk, 6 feet in diameter. Place nine golf balls inside the circle.

2. Use a colored ball (or mark a plain one) for the cue ball. Give each player a stick. Decide what order you'll play in.

3. Use the stick like a real pool cue, sliding it along your hand to push the cue ball into a golf ball.

4. The goal is to knock as many golf balls out of the circle as you can. If you knock a ball out, you get another turn, unless you knock the cue ball out of the circle as well. You can shoot until you don't knock a ball out of the circle on your turn.

5. Then the next player shoots. You have to shoot from wherever the cue ball rolls at the end of the last player's turn. If the ball goes out of the circle, you can put it wherever you want in the circle.

6. Whoever gets five balls out of the circle first wins.

Other Ways to Play

❋ Take turns every time, regardless of whether a player knocked a ball out of the circle.

❋ If you knock some balls out and the cue ball rolls out of the circle, you have to put the balls you knocked out back. The next player gets to put the cue ball anywhere in the circle.

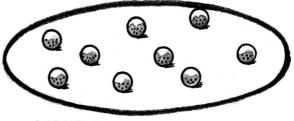

Golf Ball Billiards

Grab Tag

Number of Players: **3 or more**

What You Need: **nothing**

Where to Play: **in the yard or at the park**

The Point: **don't get tagged**

What You Do

1. Pick the first player to be IT. All of the other players run around while IT tries to tag them.

2. When IT tags you, you become IT.

3. Grab the part of your body where you were tagged and hold it while you try to tag the other players. For instance, if you were tagged on your right elbow, you have to hold that elbow in your left hand as you run around trying to tag other players.

4. Try to tag people in the most awkward spots possible. That way it'll be harder for them to tag you again.

5. When you tag another player, he or she is IT. You can stop holding the spot where you were tagged.

The Grass Is Lava

Number of Players: **3 or more**

What You Need: **playground equipment**

Where to Play: **at the park**

The Point: **don't get tagged or melted**

What You Do

1. Pick the first player to be IT. All of the other players get up on the playground equipment, or wherever they need to be to be off the ground.

2. The ground is made of lava. If you touch it, you will melt. Only IT is allowed to touch the ground.

3. If you touch the ground, scream and melt slowly. When another IT is tagged, you may rejoin the game.

4. IT chases players around the playground. IT can climb up on anything IT wants to and walk through the lava.

5. If IT tags you, you become the new IT.

The Great Foot Freeze

Number of Players: **2 or more**

What You Need: **wading pool, water, ice cubes, plastic bowl for each player**

Where to Play: **in the yard**

The Point: **get the most ice cubes in your bowl**

What You Do

1. Fill the wading pool with the water and ice cubes.

2. Give each player a plastic bowl. All of the players sit around the edge of the wading pool, with their plastic bowls and feet close to the water.

3. On "go," start picking up ice cubes with your feet and putting them in your plastic bowl. Everyone plays at the same time.

4. After a designated amount of time has passed (not so long that all the ice cubes melt!), end the game and count your ice cubes.

5. Whoever has the most ice cubes wins.

Hackey Sack

Number of Players: **4 or more**
What You Need: **hackey sack**
Where to Play: **in the yard or on pavement**
The Point: **pass around the hackey sack**

What You Do

1. Stand in a circle facing each other.

2. Throw the hackey sack underhand toward another player's feet.

3. That player kicks the hackey sack into the air and to another player. You cannot touch the hackey sack with your hands, but you may use any other body part to hit it.

4. Pass the hackey sack around the circle. When every player has kicked it, your group has one "hack." See how many hacks you can get.

5. If you drop the hackey sack, pick it up and throw it underhand toward another player's feet. You may not serve it to yourself.

6. See how many times you can get the hackey sack passed around the circle.

Hackey Sack

Hand Tennis

Number of Players: **4 or more**

What You Need: **chalk, soft bouncy ball**

Where to Play: **on pavement**

The Point: **score the most points**

What You Do

1. Draw a rectangular court on the pavement with the chalk and divide it into two sections.

2. Divide into two teams. Each team stands in one-half of the court.

3. Pick a player on each team to serve first. The server stands in the back of the court and tosses the ball (underhand) into the other team's side. The ball may not bounce in your court first.

4. The other team tries to bat the ball back to the opposing team's court. It may bounce more than once. As long as it keeps bouncing and stays within bounds, the game continues.

5. If the ball stops bouncing while inside one of the team's boundaries, the other team scores a point. If the ball is hit and lands in your court, you must return it. If you don't, the other team gets a point. If the ball goes out of bounds when it is served, the other team gets a point. If you knock the ball out of bounds on your own court, the other team gets to serve.

6. The first team to score 21 points wins. You have to be ahead by two points to win, though.

Handball

Number of Players: **2 or 4**

What You Need: **chalk, small rubber or tennis ball, wall**

Where to Play: **on pavement against a wall**

The Point: **score the most points**

What You Do

1. With the chalk, draw a handball court on the pavement in front of the wall. A regulation-size handball court is a rectangle 20 feet wide and 34 feet deep. The serving line, which runs parallel to the wall, is about 16 feet back. You can adjust these dimensions if you want.

2. Decide who'll serve first. Stand behind the serving line, bounce the ball once on the ground in front of you, then hit it into the wall with your hand. The ball must bounce off the wall and over the serving line to be considered a good serve. You get two tries to make a good serve.

3. The other player hits the ball back against the wall. It may bounce once, or you can hit it while it's still in the air.

4. Continue to take turns hitting the ball into the wall. When the ball is missed, is hit out of bounds, or is hit over the top of the wall by the player who did not serve, the server gets a point. If the server makes the mistake, the other player gets to serve.

5. You are not allowed to interfere with the other player's ability to play. Generally, this means not running in front of the other player after you've hit the ball. If you're serving and get in the way of the other player, the other player gets the ball. If you're not serving, the serve is done over.

6. The player with the most points at the end of the game wins.

7. When playing with four players, divide into two teams. The server's partner may not stand in the playing area while the ball is being served. You can take turns hitting the ball with your teammate, or you can decide that whoever is closer to it gets to hit it.

Hand Ball

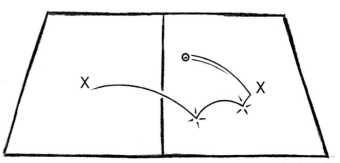

Hand Tennis

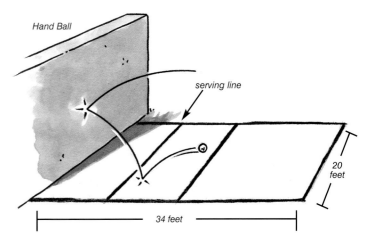

Hand Ball

serving line

20 feet

34 feet

Hide and Seek

Number of Players: **2 or more**

What You Need: **good places to hide**

Where to Play: **anywhere**

The Point: **hide well enough to not be found**

What You Do

1. Choose a home base and the first player to be IT.

2. IT stands at home base, covers ITs eyes, and counts to 50 or 100. All of the other players run away and hide.

3. When IT is finished counting, IT calls out, "Ready or not, here I come!" and looks for the other players.

4. When a player is spotted, IT must call out that player's name before chasing the player back to home base.

5. If IT gets to home base first, IT calls out, "ONE, TWO, THREE, ON (player's name)," and that player is caught. If the player gets to base first, he or she calls out, "ONE, TWO, THREE, HOME FREE."

6. When all of the players have been found, the first player to get caught becomes IT.

Other Ways to Play

✳ A hider can race home before being found.

High Fly

Number of Players: **2**

What You Need: **5 sticks, baseball, baseball mitt**

Where to Play: **in the yard or at the park**

The Point: **score the most runs**

What You Do

1. Mark the fielder's square with four of the sticks. Make it about 30 feet wide and 50 feet long. Mark the throwing line with the last stick, a little bit away from the fielder's square.

2. Decide how high the ball must be thrown, marking the height with a tree branch or telephone wire nearby.

3. The batter stands behind the throwing line and tosses the ball up to the specified height, letting it fall inside the boundary lines.

4. The fielder stands within the square and must catch the ball before it hits the ground.

5. If the ball is caught, isn't thrown high enough, or if it goes out of the fielder's square, the batter is out.

6. The batter scores a run if the fielder doesn't catch the ball.

7. After three outs, the batter and fielder switch places, and a new inning begins.

8. Play for five, seven, or nine innings.

Other Ways to Play

✻ If you've got more than two players, have a new player take the place of the batter or the fielder after each inning.

Hit the Penny

Number of Players: **2 or more**
What You Need: **penny, small rubber ball**
Where to Play: **on the sidewalk**
The Point: **hit the penny**

What You Do

1. Find a nice crack in the sidewalk. Lay the penny on the crack.

2. Stand facing the other player on another crack in the sidewalk. You should both be the same distance away from the penny.

3. Take turns bouncing the ball on the penny. If you hit it, you get a point.

4. The player with the most points wins.

Hit the Penny

Hopscotch Games

If anyone says hopscotch is a girls' game, you can tell him that it was actually invented by Roman soldiers when they guarded the roads in ancient Britain. The soldiers amused themselves by drawing hopscotch boards on the roads (sometimes they were more than 100 feet long) and hopping through them carrying heavy loads.

Hopscotch

Number of Players: **2 or more**
What You Need: **chalk, small stones**
Where to Play: **on the sidewalk**
The Point: **navigate the hopscotch course**

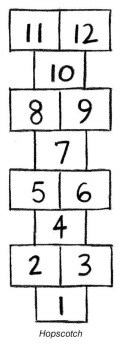

Hopscotch

What You Do

1. Mark the 12 numbered squares of the hopscotch area, following the illustration on the left. Draw a starting line in front of the first square.

2. Decide what order you'll play in. Throw the stone into square 1, jump over that square, and land with your feet in squares 2 and 3.

3. Hop all of the way to squares 11 and 12, then turn around by jumping and landing with both feet in squares 11 and 12.

4. Hop back to squares 2 and 3; pick up the stone from square 1 and jump over it.

5. If you do this without messing up (if the stone falls in the wrong square, you misplace a foot, land on the square with the stone, lose your balance, or step on a line), you get to go again.

6. Toss the stone onto square 2, and jump into squares 1, (not 2!) 3, and 4.

7. On the way back, pick up the stone while balancing on one leg in square 3.

8. Throw the stone in each square in order. When you make a mistake, the next player gets to go. Leave your stone in the last square you hopped over. All of the other players have to avoid your stone as well as their own stones.

9. The first player to reach square 12 and return wins.

Other Ways to Play

✻ Pick up your stone after you make a mistake. Hold onto it until it's your turn to play again.

Snail Hopscotch

Number of Players: **2 or more**
What You Need: **chalk**
Where to Play: **on the sidewalk**
The Point: **navigate the hopscotch course**

What You Do

1. Draw the hopscotch board below.

2. Decide what order you'll play in. You can use the board to play regular hopscotch, or you can try to hop through the whole pattern without losing your balance.

3. If you make it through the entire pattern, write your initials on one of the squares. All of the other players have to hop over that square, but you are allowed to hop in it.

Snake Hopscotch

Number of Players: **2 or more**
What You Need: **chalk, small stones (optional)**
Where to Play: **on the sidewalk**
The Point: **navigate the hopscotch course**

What You Do

1. Draw the hopscotch board below.

2. Decide what order you'll play in. You can use the board to play regular hopscotch, or you can just hop from one side to the other without touching the middle line.

3. The first player to get through the hopscotch course wins.

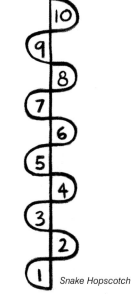

Snake Hopscotch

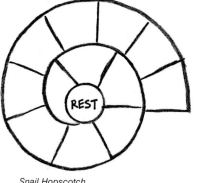

Snail Hopscotch

Hot Balloons

Number of Players: **8 or more**

What You Need: **water balloons**

Where to Play: **anywhere**

The Point: **be the last player left standing**

What You Do

1. Fill up the water balloons. Pick the first player to be the Leader. Stand in a circle around the Leader, and put all the water balloons in the middle of the circle with the Leader.

2. The Leader throws one balloon to any player. That player tosses the balloon to the player on the left. This balloon is passed around the circle counter-clockwise during the entire game.

3. Then the Leader throws the second balloon to some-one in the circle, who has to throw it back to the Leader. The Leader throws the balloon to the player on the right, who then throws it back. This balloon goes clockwise around the circle and is returned to the Leader after every pass.

4. If you drop the balloon or it bursts, sit down where you are. The balloons now must be tossed around you. The Leader substitutes another balloon and the game continues. If the Leader drops a balloon, choose a new Leader and start over.

5. The last player standing is the winner and leads the next game.

Hot Balloons

Jacks

Number of Players: **2 or more**
What You Need: **5 jacks, small bouncy ball**
Where to Play: **on the sidewalk**
The Point: **pick up all the jacks**

What You Do

1. Sit in a circle on the sidewalk. To figure out who will start the game, each player throws five jacks in the air and tries to catch as many as possible on the back of that same hand. Throw the jacks into the air again with the back of your hand and catch as many as you can in your palm. The player who has caught the most jacks goes first.

2. Toss all five of the jacks onto the pavement in front of you. Throw the ball into the air, pick up a jack with one hand, and catch the ball with the same hand before it hits the ground. If you miss, the next player gets to go. If you are successful, hold the jack you picked up in your hand and do it again. Each time pick up one jack. You must use the same hand for the whole game.

3. When you've picked up all the jacks, toss them back on the ground. Start again, this time picking up two jacks each time. (On the last play, you'll have only one jack to pick up.)

4. After you've picked up all the jacks, toss them back onto the ground. This time pick up three jacks, then the last two. On the next round, pick up four jacks, then the last one. For the final round, pick up all five jacks at once.

5. If you mess up at any point during your turn, the next player gets to go.

6. The player who gets the farthest through this progression wins.

Other Ways to Play

❖ Bounce the ball off the ground instead of throwing it into the air. You have to catch it before it bounces again.

❖ Clap your hands together after you toss the ball. Then pick up jacks and catch the ball again.

❖ Use a different hand for each round.

❖ Alternate players and see who can collect the most jacks. Pick up as many as you can on your turn.

Jump Rope Games

All you need to play jump rope is a rope to jump over. There are lots of variations from there.

Basic Jump Rope

Number of Players: **3 or more**
What You Need: **jump rope**
Where to Play: **on the sidewalk**
The Point: **see how long you can jump**

What You Do

1. Decide who will be the first player to jump. The other two players each take one end of the jump rope.

2. The players holding the jump rope start to turn it. They should stand close enough together that the top of the jump rope is higher than the jumper's head.

3. When you're ready, jump into the middle of the jump rope. Jump over it as it turns.

4. If you get tangled up in the jump rope or don't make a jump, switch places with one of the players holding it.

Other Ways to Play

❋ Jump on one foot, then the other.

❋ Jump high so that the players holding the rope can spin it around fast enough to go underneath you twice while you're in the air.

❋ Jump and bounce a ball at the same time.

❋ Let the people holding the rope speed up and slow down to try to confuse you.

❋ Sing a rhyme while jumping rope.

Double Dutch

Number of Players: **3 or more**

What You Need: **2 jump ropes**

Where to Play: **on the sidewalk**

The Point: **see how long you can jump**

What You Do

1. Decide who will be the first player to jump. The other two players take one end of each jump rope.

2. The players holding the jump ropes start to turn them. They spin one into the middle, then the other one, going the opposite direction. They must stand close enough together that the top of the jump ropes are higher than the jumper's head.

3. When you're ready, jump into the middle. Jump over both ropes as they turn.

4. If you get tangled up in one of the jump ropes or don't make a jump, switch places with one of the players holding the ropes.

Jump Rope Race

Number of Players: **2 or more**

What You Need: **start and finish line markers, a jump rope for each player**

Where to Play: **on the sidewalk**

The Point: **travel to the finish line while jumping rope**

What You Do

1. Mark the start and finish lines. Line up behind the starting line.

2. On "go," each player starts to jump rope, traveling toward the finish line.

3. If you mess up and get tangled in your rope, run back to the start line and start over.

4. The first player to cross the finish line wins.

Imitation Jump Rope

Number of Players: **4 or more**

What You Need: **jump rope**

Where to Play: **on the sidewalk**

The Point: **imitate what the player in front of you did**

What You Do

1. Pick the first two players to hold the rope. All of the other players line up.

2. The first player jumps into the middle and does something, like jumping on one leg while holding the other. If you mess up, the next player gets to do whatever he or she likes, but if you make it, the next player has to do exactly what you did.

3. Each player must imitate what the previous player did. When you make three mistakes, trade places with one of the players holding the rope.

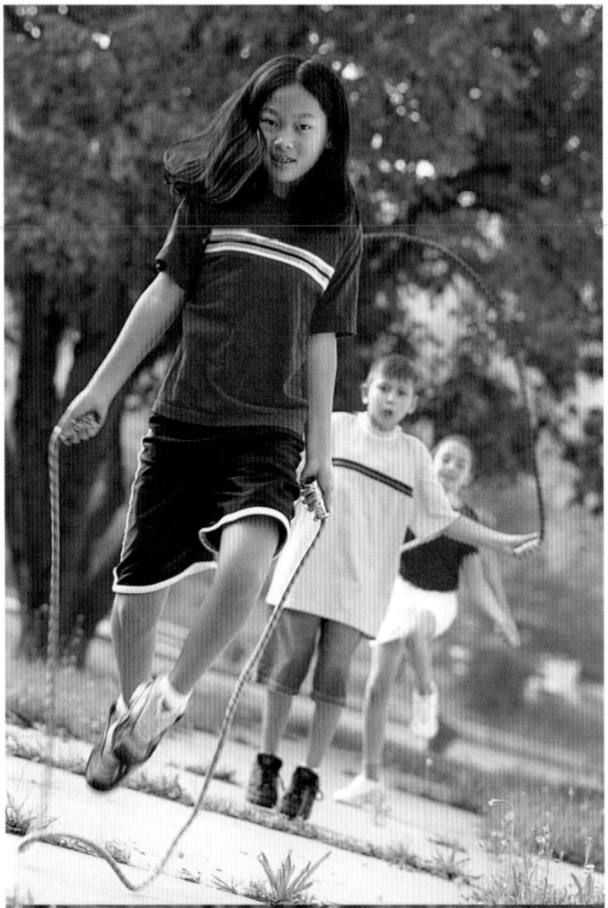

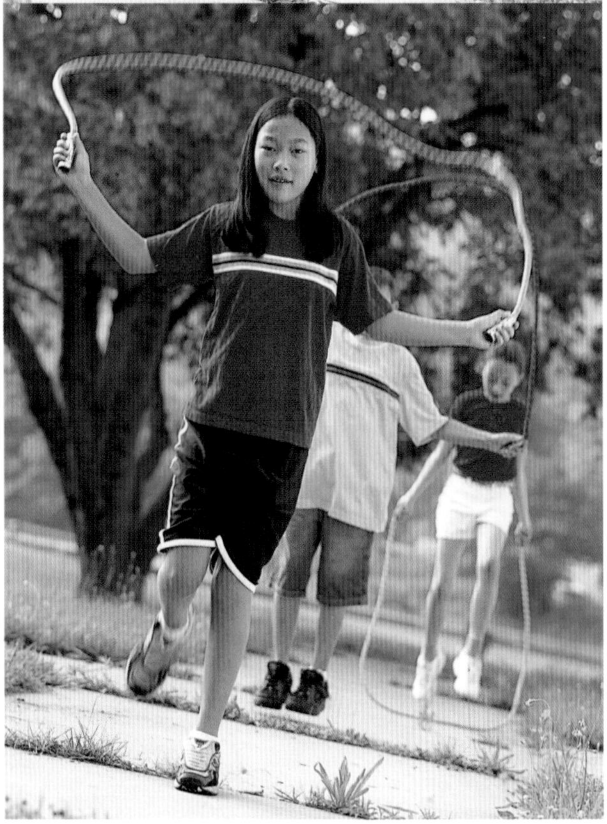

Single Jump Rope

Number of Players: **2 or more**

What You Need: **a jump rope for each player**

Where to Play: **on the sidewalk**

The Point: **see how long you can jump**

What You Do

1. All of the players get a jump rope and line up.
2. On "go," everyone starts jumping rope. See who can jump for the longest time.

Skip the Rope

Number of Players: **5 or more**

What You Need: **15-foot-long rope, soft weight to tie on the end (optional)**

Where to Play: **in the yard**

The Point: **jump over the rope each time it passes your way**

What You Do

1. Form a wide circle, with one player standing in the middle to swing the rope. If you'd like, you can tie a soft weight to the end of the rope.
2. The player in the middle swings the rope around the circle about as high as the other players' ankles.
3. Jump over the rope when it comes your way. If you miss and get hit by the rope, go into the middle of the circle. It's your turn to swing the rope.

Other Ways to Play

- The player in the middle can call out how the other players are supposed to jump over the rope. For instance, with both feet, hop and land on the left foot, keep your hands on your head, etc.

Teddy Bear Jump Rope

Number of Players: **3 or more**

What You Need: **jump rope**

Where to Play: **on the sidewalk**

The Point: **see how long you can jump**

What You Do

1. Play regular jump rope, except that the players holding the rope will be reciting the following rhyme. You have to do the actions of the rhyme when they are called.

2. The players holding the rope start to turn it. Jump in when you're ready. Once you're in the middle, the players holding the rope start to sing:

   Teddy Bear, Teddy Bear, turn around (turn around)

   Teddy Bear, Teddy Bear, touch the ground (touch the ground)

   Teddy Bear, Teddy Bear, tie your shoe (touch your shoe)

   Teddy Bear, Teddy Bear, read the news (pretend to read a newspaper)

   Teddy Bear, Teddy Bear, climb the stairs (pretend to climb the stairs)

   Teddy Bear, Teddy Bear, say your prayers (put your hands together)

   Teddy Bear, Teddy Bear, turn out the light (turn off the invisible light switch)

   Teddy Bear, Teddy Bear, say good night (say good night and hop out of the middle)

3. After you've jumped out of the middle, trade places with one of the holders and play again.

Keep Your Eye on the Ball

Number of Players: **3 or more**

What You Need: **tennis balls, water balloons, bucket, bat**

Where to Play: **anywhere**

The Point: **trick the batter into hitting a water balloon instead of the ball**

What You Do

1. Pick the first two players to start as the pitcher and the batter. All of the other players field.

2. The pitcher takes the tennis balls and water balloons to the pitching mound and hides them in the bucket.

3. The batter stands behind the plate with the bat.

4. The pitcher picks up a tennis ball or water balloon and hides it carefully so that the batter can't see which one was chosen.

5. Toss the ball or water balloon to the batter. The batter can decide whether to swing or step back.

6. If the batter gets a hit or lets three tennis balls or water balloons go by, a new player gets to bat. Don't forget to switch out the pitcher too!

Kicking Off!

Number of Players: **2 or more**

What You Need: **football**

Where to Play: **in the yard or at the park**

The Point: **come up with interesting football plays**

What You Do

1. All of the players are on the same team, playing offense against an invisible team.

2. Start the football game with a kickoff.

Keep Your Eye on the Ball

3. Teammates have to come up with spectacular plays against the invisible team.

4. Show off your runs, catches, and throws, as if your plays were going into the National Football League Hall of Fame.

5. Invent creative strategies. It's your moment to shine on the field.

Kick the Can

Number of Players: **4 or more**

What You Need: **chalk, empty can**

Where to Play: **in the yard or on pavement**

The Point: **don't get caught**

What You Do

1. Mark a circle on the ground with the chalk. Put the can inside it. Pick the first player to be IT.

2. To begin the game, one of the players kicks the can out of the chalk circle. All of the players run and hide. IT has to kick the can back into the circle and then count to 100. Then IT shouts, "Ready or not, here I come!" and goes searching for the other players.

3. When IT sees another player, IT shouts that player's name and they race back to the can. If the player kicks the can without being tagged, then he or she is safe. If the player is tagged or if IT kicks the can first, the player is caught and must stand inside the chalk circle. Unless this player is freed, he or she will be IT in the next round.

4. You can free a caught player by leaving your hiding place and kicking the can out of the circle. If you make it without being tagged by IT, you and the other player run and hide again. IT must kick the can back into the circle before searching for other players.

5. IT must find all of the players and keep at least one of them caught. That player becomes the new IT.

Other Ways to Play

- Instead of counting to 100, IT can return the can to the circle by kicking it backward, and then walk around the circle 10 times.
- A player can be rescued only three times per round.

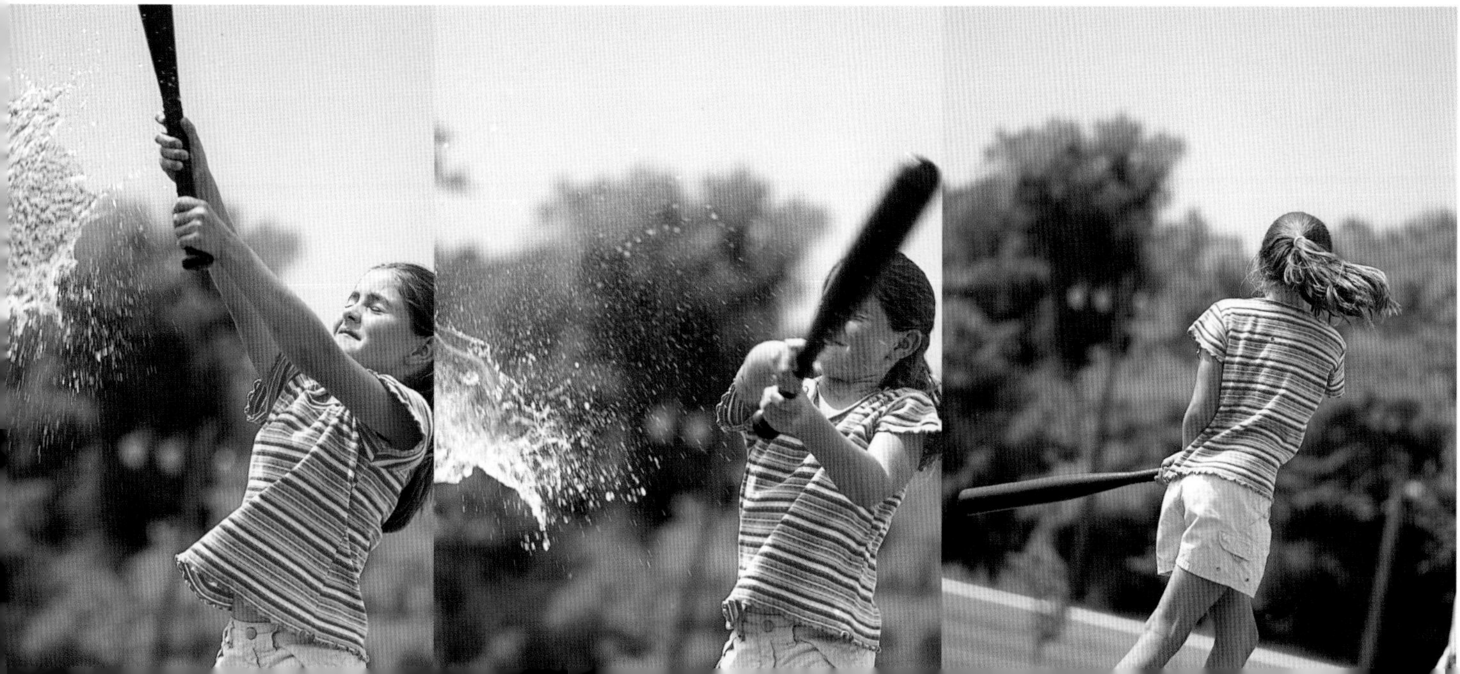

Kick Ball

Number of Players: **10 to 18**

What You Need: **bases, kick ball**

Where to Play: **in a field or on pavement**

The Point: **score the most runs**

What You Do

1. Set up the bases like a baseball diamond. The bases are usually about 25 feet apart. Make a pitcher's mound in the middle.

2. Divide into two teams and figure out which team will kick first. The other team fields, with one player pitching, one catching, and one covering each base. If you have more players, they can play shortstop or in the outfield.

3. The first player to kick steps up to home plate, and the pitcher rolls the ball to him or her. The kicker has three chances to kick the ball before getting an out. Two foul balls count as one chance.

4. After you've kicked the ball, run to first base. The fielders try to catch the ball and get you out with it. There are a few ways to get a kicker out: catch the ball in the air and before it hits the ground, throw the ball to the base before the kicker gets there, tag the runner with the ball, or hit the runner below the waist with the ball.

5. If you've safely made it onto a base, wait there while the next player kicks the ball. Then run to the next base. Make it across home plate to score a run. You can't have more than one player from your team on a base, and if a fly ball is caught, you have to go back to the base you started on.

6. After three outs, the other team gets to kick.

7. The team with the most runs wins.

Kick Ball

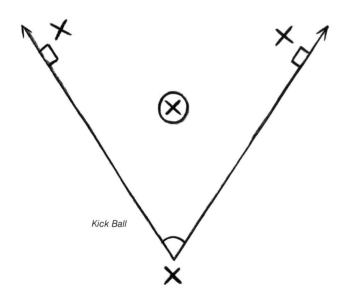

Kick Ball

Kid Olympics

Number of Players: **2 or more**

What You Need: **stuff for the games (see below), awards like old medals, certificates, cookies, or whatever you think makes a good prize**

Where to Play: **in the yard**

The Point: **win the Olympics for your country**

What You Do

1. Decide which games will make up your Kid Olympics. You can pick any games, like tumbling, water balloon toss, or the cross-yard dash. Or you can make up your own crazy games, like a crab walk or egg toss.

2. Gather all the equipment you'll need for your Kid Olympics. Have each player pick a country to represent.

3. Keep track of who wins each game. Pass out awards when the Olympics are through.

Killer Whale

Killer Whale

Number of Players: **3 or more**
What You Need: **nothing**
Where to Play: **in the pool**
The Point: **don't get eaten by the Killer Whale**

What You Do

1. Choose the first player to be the Killer Whale.

2. Get in the middle of the pool (or in the middle of the shallow end). The Killer Whale should be in the center of all the players.

3. As the game begins, the Killer Whale is a gentle, completely harmless Black Whale. All of the other players swim around in the pool. You must stay closer to the Killer Whale than you are to the sides of the pool.

4. After swimming lazily about for a while, the Killer Whale shouts out "Killer Whale!" All of the players head for the sides of the pool.

5. If you make it to the side without getting tagged by the Killer Whale, you're safe. If you get tagged, you become the new Killer Whale and the game starts over.

6. If the Killer Whale doesn't catch anyone, he or she shouts "Black Whale" and the players move back into the center and the game begins again.

Other Ways to Play

✤ Have a penny for each player. Pick one penny that has a different date from all the rest. Shuffle the pennies and have each player pick one. The player who gets the penny with the different date is the Killer Whale, but no one knows until he or she shouts "Killer Whale!"

Kings, Queens, Jacks

Number of Players: **4 or more**
What You Need: **boundary markers**
Where to Play: **in the yard or on pavement**
The Point: **be the last remaining player**

What You Do

1. Mark a circular playing area on the ground about 20 to 30 feet wide with the chalk. Outside the circle is a safe area.

2. Choose the first player to be IT. IT stands in the middle of the circle with all of the other players outside it.

3. If IT says "Kings," all of the players run straight across the circle to the other side. IT tries to catch the players as they run by. If you get caught, join IT in the center of the circle and help catch other players.

4. If IT says "Queens," all of the players have to hop across the circle on one foot. IT (and any captured players) must also hop to catch them.

5. If IT says "Jacks," no one can move until a new call is made. If you move, sit down in the safe area.

6. IT can make rapid calls to confuse the other players. Remember to keep your ears open for "Jacks!"

7. Whoever is the last remaining player wins and starts the next game as IT.

Knots

Number of Players: **5 or more**
What You Need: **nothing**
Where to Play: **anywhere**
The Point: **untangle yourselves**

What You Do

1. All of the players stand in a circle, facing each other. Everybody puts their hands into the center.

2. Take another player's hand in each of your own. You cannot hold both hands of the same player, and you cannot hold hands with the players standing next to you.

3. Once all the players are holding hands, start to untangle the knot. Step over and under other players' arms. Do not let go of each other's hands.

4. The game is over when everyone is standing in a circle again.

Knots

La Luna y las Estrellas

Number of players: **3 to 10**

What You Need: **a tree**

Where to Play: **in the yard**

The Point: **don't get tagged**

What You Do

1. Gather around a tree that casts a big shadow.

2. Pick the first player to be la Luna (the moon).

3. All of the other players are las Estrellas (the stars).

4. La Luna can't leave the tree's shadow.

5. Las Estrellas run around the tree, in and out of the shadow, while la Luna tries to tag them.

6. If la Luna tags an Estrella, that Estrella becomes the new Luna and the game starts over.

Lame Hen

Number of Players: **4 or more**

What You Need: **20 sticks, each about 2 feet long, start line marker**

Where to Play: **in the yard or on pavement**

The Point: **hop faster than the other team**

What You Do

1. Divide into two teams. Each team gets 10 sticks.

2. Line up the sticks, about 18 inches apart, like the rungs of a ladder. There should be a row for each team. Make a start line about 15 feet away.

3. Line up the teams behind the start line. Decide what order you'll race in.

4. On "go," the first player from each team hops on one foot to the sticks. You must then hop over every stick, squawking like a hen the entire way. At the end, pick up the last stick you hopped over and hop back to the beginning of the stick ladder. Put the stick down, 18 inches in front of the first stick.

5. Once the stick has been placed, the next member of your team can start hopping.

6. The first team to get back to the start line wins.

Other Ways to Play

✳ If you don't have enough players, form one team and time yourselves. Try to beat that time.

Lame Hen

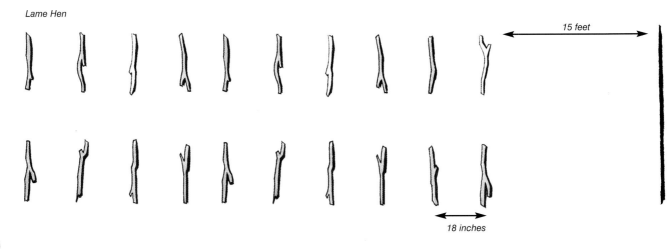

15 feet

18 inches

Lawn Furniture Obstacle Course

Number of Players: **2 or more**

What You Need: **lawn furniture, start and finish line markers, stopwatch**

Where to play: **in the yard**

The Point: **make it through the obstacle course in the least amount of time**

What You Do

1. Arrange all of the lawn furniture you can find into an obstacle course.

2. Decide whether you have to jump over, crawl under, or run around each particular piece of furniture.

3. Mark a start line and a finish line.

4. Run the race while another player times you with the stopwatch.

Other Ways to Play

✳ Get as crazy as you want with the obstacles: somersault beneath a table, do a headstand on a chair, whatever!

✳ If you don't have enough lawn furniture, use other things (or other players) to make obstacles.

Lazy Bikes

Number of Players: **2 or more**

What You Need: **chalk, a bike for each player**

Where to Play: **on the sidewalk**

The Point: **coast the farthest on your bike**

What You Do

1. Mark two lines with the chalk about 30 feet apart.

2. Line up behind the first line. On "go," start pedaling as fast as you can toward the second line.

3. As you cross the second line, stop pedaling and coast as far as you can. When you run out of momentum, stop and stand still.

4. The player who coasts the farthest wins.

Lazy Bikes

Limbo

Number of Players: **4 or more**

What You Need: **broom handle or long stick**

Where to Play: **anywhere**

The Point: **see how low you can go**

What You Do

1. Pick the first two players to hold the limbo stick (that's the broom handle or long stick). All of the other players line up behind the stick.

2. The holders each take one end of the stick and hold it up level with their chests.

3. The other players walk under the stick, bending over backward to get under it.

4. You may not touch the stick or the ground with any part of your body. (Well, obviously, you can touch the ground with your feet, but you get the point.) If you do, you're out.

5. After every player goes under the stick, the holders lower the stick and everyone goes again.

6. After all the players have been eliminated, have two players switch places with the holders and play again.

Limbo

Main Karet Gelang

Number of Players: **2 to 10**

What You Need: **badminton birdie or rubber bands tied together**

Where to Play: **in the yard**

The Point: **kick the birdie the most times**

What You Do

1. If you're using rubber bands, make sure they're wadded together and tied tightly so they won't come apart after you kick them. Toss the birdie into the air and kick it with one foot.

2. Continue to kick the birdie into the air until you miss and it lands on the ground. All of the other players count the number of times in a row you kick the birdie.

3. When you miss, give the birdie to the next player.

4. The player who kicks the birdie the most wins.

Manhunt

Number of Players: **4 or more**

What You Need: **home base**

Where to Play: **in the yard**

The Point: **get back to home base without being caught**

What You Do

1. Pick a home base, like a rock, wall, lamppost, or tree. Depending on how many players you have, choose one or more players to be the Hunted. All of the other players are Hunters. There should be more Hunters than Hunted.

2. The Hunters gather around the home base and count out loud to 100, while the Hunted run and hide.

3. When the count is up, the Hunters call out and begin their search. They must stay at least 10 feet away from the home base.

4. The Hunted try to sneak back to the home base without being seen.

5. If any of the Hunted are spotted by one of the Hunters, they immediately run back to home base, trying not to get tagged. The Hunters should work together to catch the Hunted.

6. If the Hunted get back to the home base unnoticed or untagged, they win. If the Hunted get tagged, the Hunter who tagged them wins and is the Hunted in the next game.

Marble Games

People have been playing marbles for a very long time. The rules are easy and can be adapted to play any way you like. Here are some different versions of the game. Pick one you like or make up a whole new version.

Basic Marbles

Number of Players: **2 or more**
What You Need: **chalk, marbles**
Where to Play: **on the sidewalk**
The Point: **knock the marbles out of the circle**

What You Do

1. Draw a circle on the sidewalk with the chalk. It should be about 2 or 3 feet wide. Decide what order you'll play in.

2. Each player puts the same number of marbles in the center of the circle, saving a taw or shooter marble. The taw is usually slighter larger and heavier than the other marbles. You use it to knock the other marbles out of the circle.

3. To shoot your taw, hold it as shown in the illustration and shoot it toward the marbles in the middle. You must shoot from outside of the circle.

4. Any marbles that you knock out of the circle you get to keep. Continue to shoot until you don't knock any marbles out of the circle. Leave your taw where it is, unless it rolled outside of the circle.

5. If you hit another player's taw, you get all the marbles that that player has collected so far.

6. After all the marbles have been knocked out of the circle, the player with the most marbles wins.

Shooting the Taw

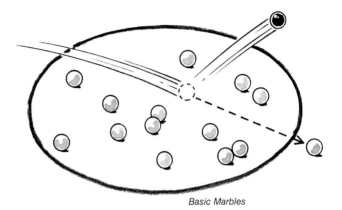

Basic Marbles

Bull's Eye

Number of Players: **2 or more**

What You Need: **chalk, marbles**

Where to Play: **on the sidewalk**

The Point: **knock the marbles out of the circle**

What You Do

1. Draw a 1-foot circle on the sidewalk with the chalk.

2. Put one marble for each player in the center of the circle.

3. Take turns standing over the circle and dropping a marble into it. You must drop the marble from eye level.

4. If your marble knocks any others out of the ring, you get to keep them. After each turn, leave your marble where it is. Use a new marble for every turn.

5. When all the marbles have been knocked out of the circle, count how many you have. The player with the most marbles wins.

Basic Marbles

Double Ring

Number of Players: **2 or more**

What You Need: **chalk, marbles**

Where to Play: **on the sidewalk**

The Point: **knock the marbles out of the circle**

What You Do

1. Draw a circle on the sidewalk with the chalk. It should be about 2 or 3 feet wide. Draw another smaller circle inside that circle. The smaller circle should be about 6 inches across.

2. Place the marbles in the inner circle. Take turns shooting your taw from the outer circle. You must knock the marbles out of both circles, and your taw must be in the outer circle at the end of your turn. Keep the marbles you successfully knock out. If the taw ends up in the inner circle, put all the marbles you just knocked out of the circle back.

3. The player with the most marbles at the end of the game wins.

Pyramid Marbles

Number of Players: **2 or more**

What You Need: **chalk, marbles**

Where to Play: **on the sidewalk**

The Point: **knock the marbles out of the circle**

What You Do

1. Draw a small circle, about 1 foot across, on the sidewalk. Decide what order you'll play in.

2. The first player builds a pyramid of marbles in the middle of the circle by placing three marbles next to each other in a shape and balancing a fourth one on top (see illustration).

3. The next player shoots his or her taw at the base of the pyramid. You get to keep any marbles that you knock out of the circle.

4. After your turn is over, set up the pyramid for the next person.

5. The player with the most marbles wins.

Pyramid Marbles

Shooting Gallery

Number of Players: **2 or more**

What You Need: **chalk, marbles**

Where to Play: **on the sidewalk**

The Point: **knock into other people's marbles**

What You Do

1. Make a line on the sidewalk with the chalk. Decide what order you'll play in.

2. The first player shoots one marble over the line.

3. The next player tries to hit that marble. If you hit it, you get to keep it. If you don't, your marble stays where it is and the next player can shoot at either one of them.

4. The player with the most marbles wins.

Marco Polo

Marco Polo

Number of Players: **3 or more**
What You Need: **nothing**
Where to Play: **in the pool**
The Point: **confuse IT and don't get tagged**

What You Do

1. Pick the first player to be IT. IT closes ITs eyes and must keep them closed for the rest of the game. All of the other players swim away.

2. When IT is ready, IT calls out "Marco." All of the other players have to respond by calling out "Polo."

3. IT follows the sound of the other players' voices and tries to tag them. IT may call out "Marco" however often IT wants, and you have to respond every time. You can swim away from IT only when IT yells "Marco."

4. When IT tags a player, that player becomes the new IT.

Monkey in the Middle

Number of Players: **3 or more**
What You Need: **a ball or Frisbee**
Where to Play: **in the yard**
The Point: **keep the ball away from the Monkey**

What You Do

1. Pick the first player to be the Monkey. The Monkey stands in between the other players.

2. The other players toss the ball or Frisbee back and forth. The Monkey tries to grab it.

3. If the Monkey intercepts the ball or Frisbee after you threw it, you become the new Monkey. If you miss a catch and the Monkey grabs the ball or Frisbee, you become the new Monkey.

Mount Ball

Number of Players: **4 or more**

What You Need: **1 ball for every 4 players**

Where to Play: **in the pool**

The Point: **complete as many passes as possible**

What You Do

1. Divide into pairs. It helps if both players are close to the same size and strength.

2. Stand about waist-deep in the shallow end of the pool. One player of each pair gets on the shoulders of the other player. The player on the bottom should hold on to the legs of the player on top for stability.

3. The two players on top start to pass the ball back and forth, counting how many successful passes they have.

4. If the ball is dropped, players switch positions so that the bottom players are on top.

5. Continue playing the game. The pair with the most successful passes wins.

Other Ways to Play

❊ After each successful pass, the players on the bottom take one step away from each other.

Nine Pins

Number of Players: **2 to 5**

What You Need: **9 empty plastic soda bottles, water, rubber ball**

Where to Play: **on the sidewalk**

The Point: **score the most points**

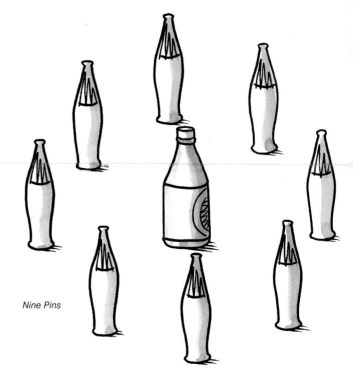

Nine Pins

What You Do

1. Fill the soda bottles with a little bit of water to help them stand up. Place the bottles as shown. The bottle in the middle is called the Jack.

2. Decide what order you'll play in. Stand at least 12 feet away from the bottles.

3. Roll the ball into the bottles, trying not to hit the Jack.

4. If you knock down one or more of the bottles on your turn without hitting the Jack, you get two points for each bottle you knocked down. Stand the bottles back up and go again.

5. If you hit one or more bottles and the Jack, you have to subtract two points from your score for every bottle you knocked over (except the Jack). Your turn is over.

6. If, in a single turn, you knock over all eight bottles without hitting the Jack, you get a 10-point bonus (in addition to the two points you scored for each bottle). Then it's the next player's turn.

7. The first player to score 20 points wins.

Other Ways to Play

❊ To make this game even more challenging, put all of the bottles less than 10 inches away from the Jack.

No-Net Tennis

Number of Players: **2**

What You Need: **chalk, tennis ball**

Where to Play: **on the sidewalk**

The Point: **score the most points**

What You Do

1. Find a flat sidewalk. Use a crack on the sidewalk for the net, or draw one with the chalk.

2. Draw boundaries 4 feet back from either side of the net.

3. Decide what order you'll play in. To serve the ball, bounce it once on your own side and then once on the other side of the net.

4. If you make a bad serve and the ball lands out of bounds or bounces twice on your own side, then the other player gets the ball.

5. If the other player catches the ball, then he or she gets to serve. If the other player misses the ball, then you get one point and go again.

6. The first player to score 15 points wins.

Other Ways to Play

❋ Use cups to catch the ball.

No-Net Tennis

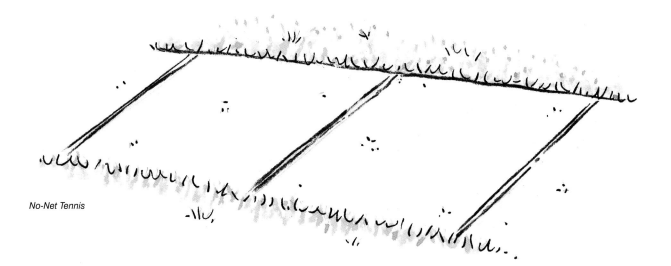

No-Net Tennis

Octopus Tag

Number of Players: **5 or more**

What You Need: **boundary markers**

Where to Play: **in the yard or at the park**

The Point: **don't get caught by the Octopus**

What You Do

1. Mark a rectangular playing area. Pick the first player to be the Octopus. All of the other players line up on one side of the playing area.

2. When the Octopus shouts "Swim!" run to the opposite side of the rectangle, trying not to get tagged.

3. If you get tagged, you must freeze in place. You are now part of the Octopus's tentacles. When other players run by you, you can reach out and tag them. Then they become part of the Octopus too. (The Octopus can run around, but the other players must stay in one place.)

4. If you make it to the opposite side of the playing area safely, wait there until the Octopus shouts "Swim!" again.

5. The last player caught starts the next game as the Octopus.

Other Ways to Play

✳ Play in the pool.

Outdoor Sculpt It!

Number of Players: **3 or more**

What You Need: **stuff around the yard**

Where to Play: **in the yard**

The Point: **get the other team to guess what you're making**

What You Do

1. Divide into two teams. One team will sculpt first, while the other team guesses what's being created.

2. The sculpting team members pick what they are going to make. After they've decided, they can't speak until the guessing team figures out what it is.

3. Make the sculpture out of stuff around the yard, like sticks, leaves, lawn chairs, rocks, and whatever else you can find. The guessing team can start guessing at any time. Once they figure out what the sculpture is, dismantle it and trade places.

4. Start out sculpting easy things, like a doghouse, then move on to more difficult things. Can you sculpt an action, like jumping?

Octopus Tag

Pavement Art

Number of Players: **1 or more**

What You Need: **chalk**

Where to Play: **on the sidewalk or in the driveway**

The Point: **create a work of art**

What You Do

1. Find a pavement crack.

2. Draw around the crack with the chalk, creating a scene around it. For example, the crack might look sort of like a tentacle. Draw a giant octopus and a sea scene.

Other Ways to Play

✳ Instead of chalk, use grass, sticks, twigs, leaves, pebbles, or anything else you find lying around in the yard to create your masterpiece.

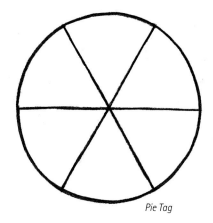

Pie Tag

Pie Tag

Number of Players: **3 or more**

What You Need: **chalk**

Where to Play: **on the sidewalk or on pavement**

The Point: **don't get tagged**

What You Do

1. Draw a six- or eight-sided pie on the ground with the chalk. Pick the first player to be IT.

2. IT stands in the middle of the pie, with the other players standing along the edges.

3. IT chases the other players, trying to tag them. You can run only on the chalk lines. If you step off the line, you're automatically IT.

4. If IT tags you, you become IT.

Pavement Art

Ping Pong Scramble

Number of Players: **2 or more**

What You Need: **several ping pong balls, 2 baskets**

Where to Play: **in the pool**

The Point: **get all the ping pong balls in your team's basket**

What You Do

1. Divide into two teams and line up on opposite sides of the pool.

2. Dump the ping pong balls into the middle of the pool. Place a basket on each side of the pool, next to the teams.

3. At "go," both teams rush to collect the ping pong balls. Each time you pick one up, you have to swim back and put it in the basket. You may not pick up more than one ping pong ball at a time.

4. The team with the most ping pong balls wins.

Other Ways to Play

❉ Put a number on each ping pong ball. The number on the ball is how much it is worth. At the end of the game, add up the number of points on the ping pong balls your team collected. For extra fun, make some of the balls worth negative points.

Poison

Number of Players: **4 to 11**

What You Need: **nothing**

Where to Play: **in the yard or at the park**

The Point: **don't get poisoned**

What You Do

1. Choose the first player to be IT. IT stands still, crosses ITs arms at the wrist, and spreads out ITs fingers. All of the other players gently hold onto one of ITs fingers.

2. IT starts the game by saying, "I went to a shop and bought a bottle of (something)." IT keeps saying different items (like root beer) until finally IT calls out, "I went to a shop and bought a bottle of POISON."

3. As soon as IT says "Poison," all of the other players let go of ITs fingers and run away. IT chases them, trying to tag one of the players.

4. The first player caught becomes the new IT.

5. If you let go of ITs finger before IT yells "poison," then you're IT.

Poison Ball

Number of Players: **4 or more**

What You Need: **a net or rope, as many balls as possible**

Where to Play: **in the pool**

The Point: **keep the balls out of your side of the pool**

What You Do

1. Stretch the net or rope across the middle of the pool. Divide into two teams. Each team gets on either side of the net with half of the balls.

2. At "go," all of the players throw the balls across the net.

3. Try to return all of the balls in your area to the other side of the net.

4. If you throw a ball out of bounds, you must go get it and return it to the pool.

5. At the end of a specified time, the team with the fewest balls on its side wins.

Poison Ball

Polybottles

Number of Players: **2 or more**

What You Need: **chalk, 3 plastic bottles one-third full of water, large lightweight ball**

Where to Play: **on the sidewalk**

The Point: **knock down all 3 bottles before the Defender can stand them back up**

What You Do

1. Mark a 7-foot circle on the sidewalk with the chalk. Pick the first player to be the Defender. The Defender puts the three bottles in the center of the circle and stands there to defend them.

2. All of the other players stand outside of the circle and take turns rolling or throwing the ball at the bottles. You can also pass the ball to each other to keep the Defender confused.

3. The Defender blocks the ball and, if he or she catches it, returns it to any of the players.

4. If a bottle falls, the Defender can stand it up but cannot touch the bottles otherwise.

5. Whoever knocks down all three bottles before they can be stood up again is the next Defender.

Prisoner's Base

Number of Players: **8 or more**

What You Need: **boundary markers**

Where to Play: **on pavement or in the yard**

The Point: **capture all the members of the other team or sneak into their prison**

What You Do

1. Mark off a playing area, 30 feet by 50 feet. Make a line down the center and mark out two opposite corners. These are the prisons.

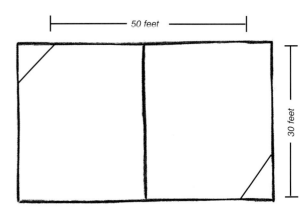

Prisoner's Base

Polybottles

2. Divide into two teams. Each team takes one side of the playing area.

3. The goal of the game is to capture all of the other team's players or to sneak into their prison when it is empty.

4. To capture other players, tag them when they are on your side of the court. They have to stand in the prison until one of their teammates comes over and tags them.

5. You can tag escaping prisoners (and those who break them out of jail) as soon as they leave the prison.

6. If you sneak into the other team's prison when it is empty, your team wins the game.

7. The game ends when all of the players on one team have been captured, or if someone from the opposite team sneaks into the empty prison without being caught.

Other Ways to Play

✳ You can rescue only one prisoner at a time.

Puss in the Corner

Number of Players: **5 or more**
What You Need: **bases**
Where to Play: **in the yard**
The Point: **don't get caught without a corner**

What You Do

1. Choose the first player to be IT. All of the other players each stand on a base. There should be a base for every player except IT.

2. Start running from base to base. There can be only one player on a base at a time. If someone runs up to your base, you have to find a new one.

3. IT tries to get to one of the empty bases before another player does.

4. If IT thinks the players have been standing too long at the bases, IT can say "All change." All of the other players have to find a new base then.

5. If you get caught without a base, you're IT.

Random Useless Fact Tag

Number of Players: **3 or more**

What You Need: **nothing**

Where to Play: **in the yard or at the park**

The Point: **don't get tagged**

What You Do

1. Pick the first player to be IT. When the game begins, IT chases the other players, trying to tag them.
2. You can be safe by calling out a random fact (like "Porcupines float in water") and touching the ground. Then slowly count out loud from 10 to one. When you reach zero, start running again.
3. You can't use a fact more than once, and you can't repeat another player's fact.
4. When IT tags someone, that player becomes the new IT and the game continues.

Other Ways to Play

* Instead of random facts, use other categories (like state names, pizza toppings, or song titles) to be safe.

Rattlesnake

Number of Players: **5 or more**

What You Need: **nothing**

Where to Play: **in the yard or at the park**

The Point: **don't let IT tag the Rattlesnake's tail**

What You Do

1. Pick the first player to be IT. All of the other players line up and hold on to each other's waists. The first player is the Rattlesnake's head, and the last player is the Rattlesnake's tail.
2. To begin the game, IT stands in front of the Rattlesnake's head. IT tries to grab on to the Rattlesnake's tail while the Rattlesnake tries to keep IT from doing so.
3. If IT grabs onto the waist of the player who is the Rattlesnake's tail, the head breaks off and that player becomes the new IT.

Other Ways to Play

* If you've got enough players, form more than one Rattlesnake. Every time a Rattlesnake loses its head, that team gets one point. The team with the fewest points wins.

Rattlesnake

Red Light, Green Light

Number of Players: **3 or more**
What You Need: **start line marker**
Where to Play: **in the yard**
The Point: **don't get caught moving on a red light**

What You Do

1. Pick the first player to be IT and mark the start line.

2. IT stands far away from all of the other players, who are lined up behind the starting line.

3. IT will call out "Green light" and turn ITs back to the players. When IT calls out "Red light" IT turns to face the players.

4. When IT calls out "Green light," everyone starts moving toward IT.

5. As soon as IT calls out "Red light" and turns around, everyone has to freeze.

6. Anyone that IT catches moving after the red light is called has to go back to the beginning.

7. When IT calls out "Green light," all of the players start moving again.

8. The first player to touch IT wins and gets to be IT in the next game.

Red Light, Green Light

Crab Relay Race

Number of Players: **4 or more**
What You Need: **start and finish line markers**
Where to Play: **in the yard or at the park**
The Point: **cross the finish line first**

What You Do

1. Mark the start and finish lines. Divide into two or more teams, depending on how many players you have.

2. Decide what order your team will race in. Line up behind the start line. Lie on your back and push yourself off the ground with your hands and feet. This is the position you will race in.

3. On "go," the first player from each team crab walks to the finish line and back.

4. When you return to the start line, tag the hand of the next player. That player crab walks to the finish line and back.

5. Do this until every member of your team has crab walked.

6. The first team to crab walk across the finish line wins the race.

Basic Relay Race

Number of Players: **4 or more**
What You Need: **start and finish line markers**
Where to Play: **in the yard or at the park**
The Point: **cross the finish line first**

What You Do

1. Mark the start and finish lines. Divide into two or more teams, depending on how many players you have.

2. Decide what order your team will race in. Line up behind the start line.

3. On "go," the first player from each team runs to the finish line and back.

4. When you return to the starting line, tag the hand of the next player. That player runs to the finish line and back.

5. Do this until every member of your team has run. The first team to cross the finish line wins the race.

One-Legged Relay Race

One-Legged Relay Race

Number of Players: **4 or more**

What You Need: **start and finish line markers**

Where to Play: **in the yard or at the park**

The Point: **cross the finish line first**

What You Do

1. Mark the start and finish lines. Divide into two or more teams, depending on how many players you have.

2. Decide what order your team will race in. Line up behind the start line.

3. On "go," the first player from each team hops to the finish line and back.

4. When you return to the start line, tag the hand of the next player. That player hops to the finish line and back.

5. Do this until every member of your team has hopped.

6. The first team to cross the finish line wins the race.

Soap Relay Race

Number of Players: **4 or more**

What You Need: **start and finish line markers, bar of soap for each team, water**

Where to Play: **in the yard or at the park**

The Point: **cross the finish line first**

What You Do

1. Mark the start and finish lines. Divide into two or more teams, depending on how many players you have.

2. Decide what order your team will race in. Line up behind the start line. Get the soap wet and give it to the first player from each team.

3. On "go," the first player from each team runs to the finish line and back.

4. When you return to the starting line, hand the soap to the next player. That player runs to the finish line and back.

5. Do this until every member of your team has run. The first team to cross the finish line wins the race.

Water Relay Race

Number of Players: **4 or more**

What You Need: **start and finish line markers, buckets, water**

Where to Play: **in the yard or at the park**

The Point: **cross the finish line first**

What You Do

1. Mark the start and finish lines. Divide into two or more teams, depending on how many players you have. Fill one bucket with water for each team.

2. Decide what order your team will race in. Line up behind the start line.

3. On "go," the first player from each team grabs the water bucket and runs to the finish line and back. Don't spill any of the water.

4. When you return to the start line, hand the next player the water bucket. That player runs to the finish line and back with the water bucket.

5. Do this until every member of your team has run.

6. The first team to cross the finish line wins the race. Your bucket must still be full of water for your team to win.

Roly Poly

Number of Players: **3 or more**

What You Need: **bat, small rubber ball or tennis ball**

Where to Play: **in the yard or at the park**

The Point: **get up to bat**

What You Do

1. Pick the first player to bat. All of the other players will field.

2. The batter stands at home base (you don't need a marker or anything for this), throws the ball into the air, and hits it on its way back down. If you don't hit it, try again until you do.

3. If the batter hits a pop fly and a fielder catches it, that player is up to bat.

4. If the ball bounces and a fielder catches it, the batter lays the bat on the ground. The fielder stays right where he or she is and throws or rolls the ball toward the bat.

5. If the ball hits the bat, the fielder gets to bat. If the ball bounces up off the bat and the batter catches it before it bounces again, the batter hits again.

Roly Poly

91

Running Across

Number of Players: **9 or more**

What You Need: **nothing**

Where to Play: **in the yard or at the park**

The Point: **be the last player tagged**

What You Need

1. Pick the first player to be IT. IT stands in the middle of the playing area. All of the other players form two teams facing each other, with IT in the middle.
2. On "go," both sides rush across the playing area to the opposite side while IT tries to tag as many players as possible.
3. Any player who gets tagged stands in the middle and helps IT tag other players.
4. The game continues until there is only one player left who has not been tagged. That player is IT in the next game.

Running Bases

Number of Players: **3 or more**

What You Need: **boundary markers, 2 baseball gloves, baseball or tennis ball**

Where to Play: **in the yard**

The Point: **steal bases without getting tagged**

What You Do

1. Set up the boundary lines about 60 feet apart. Decide which two players will be the fielders first. They each stand on a boundary line. All of the other players are runners.
2. The runners stand at one of the boundary lines and the two other players start to play catch. The runners try to cross the boundary line while the fielders are playing catch. The fielders will try to tag the runners before they can make it across the boundary line.
3. Runners start running from boundary line to boundary line as soon as they want. Tagged runners are out.

Other Ways to Play

* After a runner is tagged three times, he or she switches places with one of the fielders.

Running Bases

Safety Tag

Number of Players: **10 or more**

What You Need: **bases, foam balls**

Where to Play: **in the yard or at the park**

The Point: **don't get tagged**

What You Do

1. Spread the bases around the playing area. There should be one base for every three players.

2. Pick the first players to be IT. There should be one IT for every five players. Give each of the ITs a ball.

3. The ITs try to tag the other players with their balls. You can throw the ball at another player, aiming below the waist, or you can tag another player with the ball.

4. You're safe if you're standing on a base, but if another person runs up to your base, you have to leave. Only one player is allowed on a base at any time.

5. If you get tagged, you become IT. The IT who tagged you must give you the ball and then join the other players.

Sardines

Number of Players: **4 or more**

What You Need: **good places to hide**

Where to Play: **in the yard**

The Point: **squash as many players into a single hiding space as possible**

What You Do

1. Choose the first player to hide. All of the other players cover their eyes at a starting point and count to 100.

2. The player hiding runs away and finds a place to hide.

3. When the other players are done counting, everyone goes to look for the hiding player.

4. Each player who finds the hiding spot must squeeze into the hiding spot.

5. The last player to find the hiding spot is chased back to the starting point by the rest of the players who are hiding there.

6. The last player becomes the next player to hide.

Sardines

Shadow Tag

Number of Players: **3 or more**

What You Need: **brightly colored clothes or reflective tape**

Where to Play: **a safe, dark street with streetlights**

The Point: **keep your shadow safe from other players**

What You Do

1. Make sure that all of the players are wearing brightly colored shirt or several pieces of reflective tape so that they can easily be seen by anyone in a car.

2. Pick the first player to be IT.

3. IT chases the other players, trying to step on their shadows. If a player is casting more than one shadow, the darkest shadow is the one IT has to tag.

4. You can be safe by hiding your shadow in another shadow.

5. If IT tags you, you become the new IT.

Other Ways to Play

❋ If it's a sunny enough day to cast good shadows, you can play this game during the day in your yard.

Shark and Minnows

Number of Players: **5 or more**

What You Need: **nothing**

Where to Play: **in the pool**

The Point: **don't get eaten by the Shark**

What You Do

1. Pick the first player to be the Shark. All of the other players are Minnows.

2. The Minnows line up on one side of the pool, either out of the water or touching the side of the pool. The Shark swims around in the middle.

3. When the Shark yells "Swim!" all of the Minnows jump into the water and swim as fast as they can toward the other side of the pool.

4. The Shark swims around, tagging as many Minnows as possible.

5. If you get caught, stay in the middle of the pool with the Shark and help tag other Minnows.

6. The game continues until all the Minnows are caught. The last Minnow caught becomes the new Shark.

Sharks and Jets

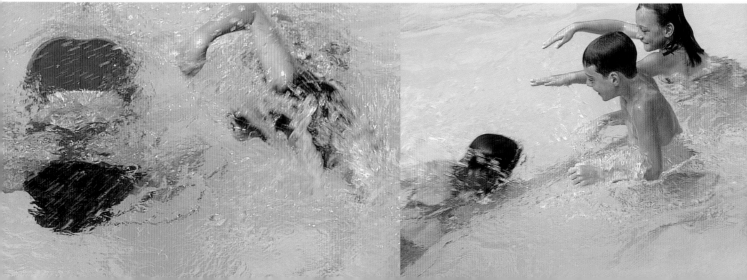

Sharks and Jets

Number of Players: **5 or more, plus a referee**

What You Need: **whistle**

Where to Play: **in the pool**

The Point: **get everybody on the same team**

What You Do

1. Divide into two teams and pick a referee. One team is the Sharks, the other is the Jets. Give the referee the whistle.

2. Line up in the shallow end of the pool, about 5 feet apart, facing each other.

3. The referee blows the whistle and calls out either "Sharks!" or "Jets!" Whichever team the referee calls chases the other team.

4. If you get tagged, join the other team.

5. The referee can blow the whistle at any time, reversing who chases whom.

6. Play until all of the players are on the same team.

Shout Out

Number of Players: **8 or more**

What You Need: **blindfold, treasure (like a ball, shoe, or water bottle)**

Where to Play: **in the yard or at the park**

The Point: **capture the treasure**

What You Do

1. Pick the first two players to be the referee and treasure keeper. All of the other players sit in a circle around the treasure keeper. The referee stands outside the circle.

2. The treasure keeper puts on the blindfold and places the treasure on the ground nearby.

3. The referee points to one of the players in the circle. That player sneaks up on the treasure keeper as quietly as possible and tries to steal the treasure.

4. The treasure keeper points in the direction of any sound. The treasure keeper cannot point wildly about. You must point directly at the place where you heard the sound.

5. The referee shouts "Out!" when the treasure keeper points at the player approaching. That player returns to the circle and the referee picks a different player to try to steal the treasure.

6. The player who captures the treasure becomes the next treasure keeper. The previous treasure keeper becomes the referee and the referee joins the circle as a player.

Sidewalk Golf

Number of Players: **2 or more**

What You Need: **chalk, game piece (like a small stone or coin—something that won't roll)**

Where to Play: **on the sidewalk**

The Point: **get the lowest score**

What You Do

1. Give each player a piece of chalk. Design your own golf hole on the sidewalk. Each hole should have a small circle that the game piece will fit in, a larger outline that marks the boundaries, a teeing line on the opposite side of the small circle, and of course, obstacles. To make obstacles, draw shapes inside the boundaries and label what kind of obstacles they are. (For instance, make a few sand traps, tiger pits, and black holes.)

2. Decide which order the golf holes will be played. All of the players line up behind the teeing line of the first hole.

3. Toss your game piece at the small circle. If it doesn't make it into the circle on the first try, move to where the marker is and throw or shoot it again. If you fall in one of the traps, go back to the teeing line and start again. Count the number of throws it takes you to get the marker in the circle.

4. Play until you make it in the hole, keeping track of the number of tries you needed. After all of the players make it in the hole, move to the next hole and do it again.

5. At the end of the game, add up how many tries you needed for each hole. The player with the lowest score wins.

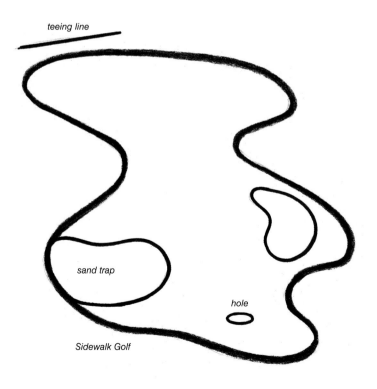

teeing line

sand trap

hole

Sidewalk Golf

Simon Says

Number of Players: **6 or more**

What You Need: **nothing**

Where to Play: **anywhere**

The Point: **listen closely to what Simon says**

What You Do

1. Choose the first player to be Simon. All of the other players stand facing Simon.

2. Simon tells the players what to do by saying "Simon says do this," and then shows everyone what they're supposed to do. For example, Simon might say, "Simon says do this," and then touch his or her toes. All of the players have to touch their toes.

3. If Simon doesn't say, "Simon says" before saying "do this," then don't move.

4. If you move when you're not supposed to, you're out. The last player out gets to be Simon in the next round.

Other Ways to Play

�֎ Instead of doing the action, Simon can just call out the action, like "Simon says hop around in a circle on your left foot."

Single Football

Number of Players: **4 or more**

What You Need: **start line marker, dodge ball, tree**

Where to Play: **in the yard or at the park**

The Point: **run from the start line to the tree and back again**

What You Do

1. Mark the start line on the ground a good distance away from the tree.

2. Pick the first player to be the runner. The runner stands behind the start line with the ball. All of the other players are fielders and can stand anywhere in the playing area.

3. The runner throws the ball up and forward, then runs to the tree and touches it. All of the other players try to catch the ball while the runner races back to the start line.

4. If you catch the ball, stay where you are and toss it at the runner's knees, or pass it to one of the other players.

5. If you hit the runner with the ball before he or she crosses the start line, you get to be the new runner. If you don't, the runner gets the ball back and plays again.

Single Football

Skully

Number of Players: **2 to 6**

What You Need: **chalk, shooter for each player, like a bottle cap or small stone**

Where to Play: **on pavement or the sidewalk**

The Point: **get through all the Skully bases**

What You Do

1. Draw the Skully court on the sidewalk with the chalk, following the illustration below. The sides of the court should each be 3 feet long. In the Pit, make a big X going from one corner to another. Number all of the other squares as indicated. You have to get your shooter in each square in order.

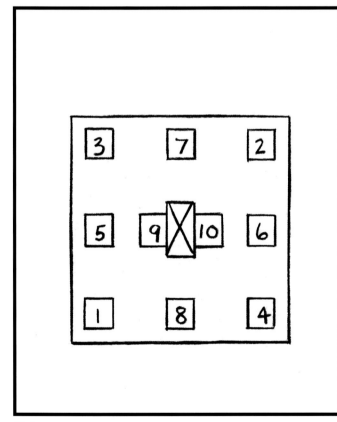

Skully

2. Decide what order you'll play in. Place your shooter in the middle of the X in the Pit. Use your finger to flick it toward square one. If you make it in the square (if your shooter is touching the lines of the square, it counts as in), you can move the shooter to anywhere within that square. Then flick it toward the next square.

3. If you miss, leave your shooter where it is and let the next player go. You'll begin your next turn from there. If you knock your shooter out of bounds, put it back in at the point where it went out. If your shooter lands on part of the X in the Pit, you have to put it back in the last square you were on.

4. If your shooter goes out of bounds twice or lands in the open space of the Pit (not on the X), you have to start all over on your next turn. If your shooter lands on the boundary lines of the Pit, it counts as being in the Pit.

5. If you hit another person's shooter, you get to move forward to the next box.

6. The first player to get through all the squares in order wins.

Other Ways to Play

✳ After you make it through the entire sequence, your shooter becomes a Killer. When it's your turn, just shoot at other people's shooters. If you hit someone three times, he or she is out of the game. If someone hits you, he or she becomes a Killer too.

✳ There are many different versions of the Skully board, and a lot of different rules that people have made up over time. Make sure everyone agrees on the rules before starting.

Slam Ball

Number of Players: **4 or more**
What You Need: **chalk, dodge ball**
Where to Play: **on pavement**
The Point: **get everybody else out**

What You Do

1. Make a line on the pavement with the chalk. Decide what order you'll play in.

2. The first two players stand on either side of the line, 8 to 10 feet apart. All of the other players line up off to the side.

3. The first player walks up to the dividing line, puts one foot over it, and bounces the ball hard toward the other player. This is the Slam, and there are certain rules it has to meet (see the list of Slam Rules). If you don't, you get to try it again.

4. The second player catches the ball before it hits the ground, runs and puts a foot over the dividing line, and bounces the ball back at the first player.

5. When you mess up, go to the end of the line. The first person in the line takes your place.

6. Whoever can beat everybody in the line in a single turn wins.

Slam Rules

A Slam that violates any of the following rules (except the last one) must be re-Slammed. The players waiting in line get to referee.

Haystack: The ball bounces straight up in the air instead of toward the other player.

Skidder: The ball bounces nearly parallel to the ground, making it impossible to catch.

Sider: The ball bounces off to the side instead of toward the other player.

Cherry bomb: The ball hits the other player in the face or head. If this happens, your turn is over.

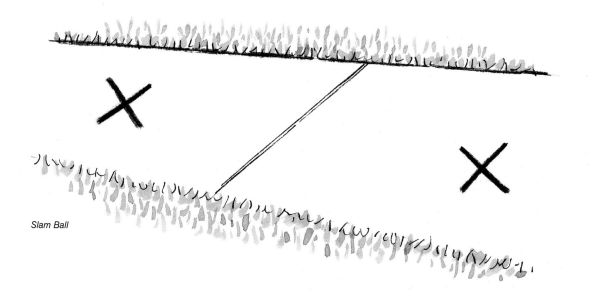

Slam Ball

Slap Ball

Number of Players: **2 or more**

What You Need: **rubber ball**

Where to Play: **in the yard**

The Point: **don't drop the ball**

What You Do

1. All of the players stand in a circle. Begin the game by hitting the ball, with both palms flat, into the air.

2. Hit the ball when it comes your way, trying to keep it airborne for as long as possible. Count how many times in a row you hit it.

3. Start over when the ball hits the ground.

Other Ways to Play

✳ To make the game more challenging, have someone call a hitting style. For instance, if the hitting style is "Jump," everyone has to jump before hitting the ball.

✳ Play slap ball around a sprinkler.

Slow Kid's Revenge

Number of Players: **4 or more**

What You Need: **boundary markers**

Where to Play: **in the yard or at the park**

The Point: **be the last player tagged**

What You Do

1. Mark the start and finish line, and mark boundaries along the sides.

2. All of the players line up behind the starting line.

3. On "go," everyone races to the finish line. The last player to cross it goes and stands in the middle of the playing area.

4. All of the other players line up behind the start line again.

5. On "go," the players race across the playing area. The player in the middle runs around and tries to tag as many of the other players as possible. The runners can slow down, speed up, run in circles, or whatever. The only two things they cannot do are stop running or go out of bounds. Once they cross the finish line they are safe.

6. Tagged players join the player in the middle after they've been caught. Then they try to tag the remaining players as well.

Slap Ball

Soft Fuzzy Things of Death

Number of Players: **4 or more**

What You Need: **boundary markers, Soft Fuzzy Things of Death**

Where to Play: **in the yard**

The Point: **get everyone on the same team**

What You Do

1. Mark a large, circular boundary and divide into two teams. Each team gets half of the Soft Fuzzy Things of Death.

2. One team goes into the center of the playing area. The other team stands outside of the circle.

3. Start throwing the Soft Fuzzy Things of Death at the other team. You have to aim below the neck. Everyone plays at the same time.

4. If you get hit, join the other team. If you catch a Soft Fuzzy Thing of Death, the player who threw it has to join your team.

5. Keep playing until all of the players are on the same team.

How to Make a Soft Fuzzy Thing of Death

What You Need

Scissors

Cardboard

Yarn

Tape

What You Do

1. Have all of the players help make a bunch of Soft Fuzzy Things of Death. To make one, cut two cardboard circles with a hole in the middle, so that each piece looks like a doughnut. The cardboard circles should be about 1½ to 2 inches wide (see template).

2. Put the two cardboard circles together. Secure the tail of the yarn to one of the circles of cardboard with a piece of tape (see figure 1). Wind the yarn around and around the cardboard circle. Wind it until the hole in the middle of the cardboard is completely filled in.

3. Cut the yarn wrapped around the outside of the cardboard circle (see figure 2). Carefully pull the two circles apart a little bit. Tie a piece of yarn tightly around the middle of the yarn wad in between the cardboard circles.

4. Pull off the cardboard circles. Congratulations! You've made a Soft Fuzzy Thing of Death. Now make a lot more.

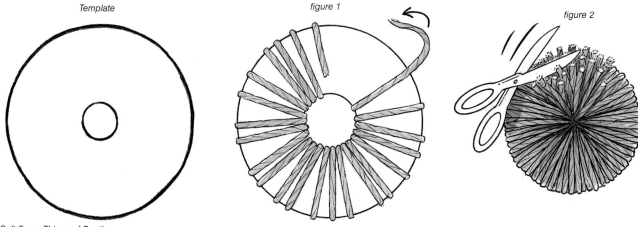

Template

figure 1

figure 2

Soft Fuzzy Things of Death

Sponge Tag

Number of Players: **3 or more**

What You Need: **water bucket, big sponge**

Where to Play: **in the yard**

The Point: **don't get tagged by the wet sponge**

What You Do

1. Put the water buckets in the middle of the playing area. Pick the first player to be IT.

2. IT soaks the sponge in water and chases all of the other players, trying to tag them with the wet sponge. IT can throw the sponge at a player or use it to tag a player.

3. If you get hit or tagged with the sponge, you're IT. Soak the sponge in water whenever it gets too dry.

4. Keep playing until everyone is very wet.

Other Ways to Play

✽ If you have more than one sponge, have more than one player be IT at a time.

Sponge Tag

Sprinkler Games

What's the best way to cool off on a hot summer day when you can't get to the pool? Sprinklers—they aren't just for watering the lawn anymore.

Car Wash

Number of Players: **2 or more**
What You Need: **sprinkler**
Where to Play: **in the yard**
The Point: **get wet**

What You Do

1. Set up the sprinkler in the middle of the playing area.
2. Pretend that you're a really dirty automobile. Run through the sprinkler until you're clean.

Water Limbo

Number of Players: **2 or more**
What You Need: **sprinkler**
Where to Play: **in the yard**
The Point: **get wet**

What You Do

1. Pick up the sprinkler and hold it out in front of you. The other players walk beneath the sprinkler, bending over backward to get underneath. They may not touch the ground with their hands.
2. After each player makes it under the sprinkler, hold it a bit lower and play again. Keep lowering the sprinkler until you've gone as low as you can go.
3. Trade places so that everyone gets a turn to go underneath the sprinkler.

Sprinkler Volleyball

Number of Players: **2 or more**
What You Need: **sprinkler, volleyball or similar-size ball**
Where to Play: **in the yard**
The Point: **get wet**

What You Do

1. Set up the sprinkler in the middle of the playing area and divide into teams. The players stand on either side of it. It's the volleyball net.
2. Punch the ball back and forth over the sprinkler. If the ball lands on the ground, the other team gets a point.
3. The team with the most points wins.

Freezer Game

Number of Players: **2 or more**
What You Need: **sprinkler**
Where to Play: **in the yard**
The Point: **get wet**

What You Do

1. Set up the sprinkler in the middle of the playing area. Pick the first player to be IT. All of the other players dance around the sprinkler.
2. When IT yells "Freeze" stop moving and let the sprinkler splash you. The first person to move or flinch is IT.

Spud

Number of Players: **5 or more**

What You Need: **dodge ball**

Where to Play: **in the yard or on pavement**

The Point: **don't spell Spud**

What You Do

1. Pick the first player to be IT. IT stands in the middle of the playing area with the ball. All of the other players gather around.

2. IT tosses the ball into the air, calling another player's name. If your name is called, you must catch the ball while all of the other players run away.

3. As soon as you catch the ball, yell "Spud!" All of the other players freeze where they are.

4. Take three giant steps toward another player and throw the ball at that player's feet. The other player may not move to avoid getting hit by the ball.

5. If the ball hits the player, that player gets an "S" and becomes IT. If the ball misses the player, you get an "S" and stay IT. If the player moves to avoid the ball, he or she gets an "S."

6. The game continues until a player spells "Spud." When you spell Spud, you're out.

7. The last player still in the game wins.

Standoff

Number of Players: **2 or more**

What You Need: **nothing**

Where to Play: **in the yard**

The Point: **don't lose your balance**

What You Do

1. Pair up so that every player has a partner.

2. Stand with your feet together, facing your partner at arm's length. Put your arms out and your hands, palms up, on your partner's hands.

3. Try to knock each other off balance. You can touch only each other's hands.

4. If you move one of your feet, your partner gets a point. If you move both of your feet, your partner gets two points. If you fall over or into your partner, he or she gets three points. If you both lose your balance, nobody gets any points.

5. The player with the high score wins.

Other Ways to Play

✳ Play tournament style. The winners from each pair play each other.

✳ Play this game in the pool.

Spud

Statues

Number of Players: **4 or more**

What You Need: **nothing**

Where to Play: **anywhere**

The Point: **pose as the best statue**

What You Do

1. Pick the first player to be the Sculptor.

2. The Sculptor twirls each player around, one at a time. When the Sculptor stops twirling you, freeze into a statue.

3. Hold your position until all the players have been turned into statues.

4. The Sculptor picks the best statue. That player is the next Sculptor.

Other Ways to Play

❊ The Sculptor can tell the players what sorts of sculptures they should be, like animals.

Steal the Bacon

Number of Players: **6 or more**

What You Need: **boundary markers, "bacon" (a hat or water bottle)**

Where to Play: **in the yard**

The Point: **steal the bacon and get the most points**

What You Do

1. Pick the first player to be the referee. Mark a playing area and put the bacon in the center.

2. Divide into two teams and count off so every player has a number. The teams line up on opposite sides of the playing area, standing out of bounds.

3. The referee calls out a number. The player from each team with that number rushes toward the bacon.

4. If you reach the bacon first, grab it and run back to your side before the other player tags you. If the other player gets the bacon first, try to tag him or her.

5. If you get the bacon back to your team, your team gets a point. If you get tagged, the other team gets a point. If the other player has the bacon and you tag him or her, your team gets a point.

6. The team with the most points wins.

Stickball

Number of Players: **6 or more**

What You Need: **chalk, bases, stick or bat, tennis ball**

Where to Play: **in a field or at the park**

The Point: **score more runs than the other team**

What You Do

1. Mark four bases, just like in baseball. Generally, the bases are about 25 feet apart, but you can adjust this to fit your playing area. Mark a pitcher's mound, a batter's cage, and foul lines with the chalk.

2. Divide into two teams and decide which one will be at bat first. The other team will field. The team at bat decides which order they'll hit in.

3. The fielding team should have a pitcher, someone to cover first base, and someone to cover second and third base. If you have enough players, you've got an outfielder.

4. The pitcher bounces the tennis ball once to the batter, who tries to hit it. If you swing and miss, you get a strike. If you hit two fouls, you get a strike. If you get three strikes, you're out. There is no such thing as a walk in this game.

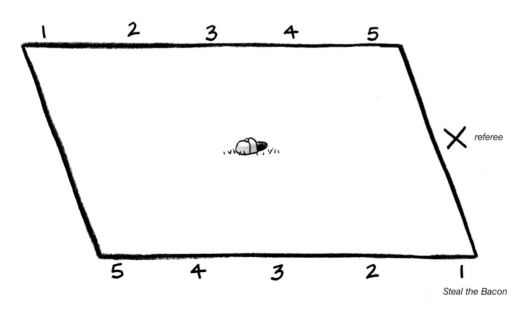

Steal the Bacon

5. If you hit the ball, sprint to first base. If the ball is caught before it hits the ground, you're out. If the ball is thrown to the player at the base you're running toward or you are tagged with it, you're out. If you make it to the base, stay there until one of your team-mates hits the ball. Then run to the next base. When you cross home plate, you score a run for your team.

6. After three outs, the teams switch places.

7. If your team is up to bat and all the players on your team are on bases, you get a ghost runner. The team member closest to home plate goes back to bat, and a ghost runner takes his or her place. Ghost runners score like any other team member but cannot be tagged out.

8. There are no home runs in stickball. If you hit the ball out of the park or in an area that's difficult to retrieve (like inside of a tall fence with a big dog), it's an automatic out and you have to go get the ball.

9. The team with the most runs wins.

Stickball

Still Pond

Number of Players: **5 or more**
What You Need: **nothing**
Where to Play: **in the pool**
The Point: **don't get caught moving**

What You Do

1. Pick the first player to be the referee. All of the other players line up on one side of the pool, touching the edge. The referee stands at the opposite end of the pool.

2. The referee closes his or her eyes and counts out loud to 10. All of the other players start swimming toward the referee's end of the pool.

3. When the referee reaches 10, he or she opens his or her eyes and calls out "Still pond!" All of the other players have to stop swimming and float in place. Any player that the referee catches moving forward has to go back to the beginning.

4. After a few minutes, the referee says "Go" and closes his or her eyes and counts to 10 again. All of the other players start swimming.

5. The first player to get to the other side of the pool is the referee in the next round.

Other Ways to Play

❉ The referee can shout "Still pond!" without counting to 10 first.

❉ You can't touch the bottom or the side of the pool to keep yourself from moving.

Stoopball

Number of Players: **2 or more**

What You Need: **small rubber ball or a tennis ball**

Where to Play: **against a stoop**

The Point: **score the most points by bouncing a ball off steps**

What You Do

1. Stand at least 5 feet from the stoop. Throw the ball at one of the stairs, trying to bounce it back so that you can catch it.

2. If the ball bounces on the steps normally and you catch it, you get 10 points. If the ball bounces on the ground once before you catch it, you get five points.

3. If you hit the corner of the stairs and catch the ball, you get 100 points.

4. If you miss the ball, drop it, or catch it after two or more bounces, it's the next player's turn.

5. The first player to score 500 or 1,000 points wins.

Sweatshirt Relay

Number of Players: **6 or more**

What You Need: **a sweatshirt for each team**

Where to Play: **in the pool**

The Point: **win the race**

What You Do

1. Divide into teams for this relay race. All of the players stand in the shallow end of the pool.

2. Give each team a sweatshirt. Decide what order your team will run in.

3. On "go," the first runners for each team dip their sweatshirts into the water, getting them completely wet. Then they must put on the sweatshirts and race to the opposite side of the pool and back.

4. When your teammate comes back, put on the sweatshirt and race to the other side of the pool and back. The sweatshirt must be completely on before you can start running.

5. The first team to have all its members make it back to the starting point wins.

Hints

❉ The fastest way to get the sweatshirt from one player to the other is to have both players lean toward each other and hold hands with their arms outstretched. The sweatshirt can then be pulled off one and onto the other by another teammate.

5 points

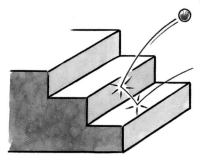

10 points

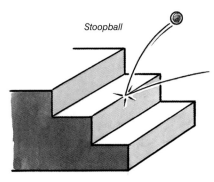

Stoopball

100 points

Tag

Number of Players: **3 or more**

What You Need: **boundary markers (optional)**

Where to Play: **in the park or backyard**

The Point: **don't get tagged**

What You Do

1. Choose the first player to be IT. Whoever is IT chases all of the other players around, trying to tag one of them.

2. If you get tagged, you're the next IT.

3. If you want, make boundaries for the game. No one is allowed to leave the boundaries.

Other Ways to Play

❋ Use some of these additional rules when you play. Make sure that everybody agrees to them:

No Tag Backs: If you've just been tagged by IT, you can't reach out and tag the player who just got you.

Safety Zones: Mark a safety zone or two. Anyone standing in one can't be tagged.

Squat Tag: Players being chased can squat down when they're about to be tagged. They are off limits until they stand up again.

Tag

Three-Legged Race

Three-Legged Race

Number of Players: **8 or more**

What You Need: **start and finish line markers, bandannas**

Where to Play: **in the yard or at the park**

The Point: **cross the finish line first**

What You Do

1. Mark the start and finish lines.

2. Pair off so that everyone has a partner. It helps if partners are close to the same size.

3. Stand next to your partner and use the bandanna to tie your inside legs together at the ankle.

4. Line up behind the start line.

5. On "go," everyone runs to the finish line.

6. The first pair to cross the finish line wins the race.

Tiger and Leopard

Number of Players: **10 or more**
What You Need: **start and finish line markers**
Where to Play: **in the yard or at the park**
The Point: **don't get caught by the Tiger**

What You Do

1. Divide into two teams. One team is Tigers, the other is Leopards.

2. Mark the start and finish lines. Line up behind the start line, pairing off so each Leopard is standing behind a Tiger.

3. Chant "A Tiger, a Leopard / A Leopard, a Tiger / One of them crouches / The other jumps over."

4. When you chant "A Tiger, a Leopard," all of the Tigers crouch down. When you chant "One of them crouches," all of the Leopards put their hands on the Tigers' shoulders.

5. When you chant "The other jumps over," the Leopards leapfrog over the Tigers and race to the finish line.

6. The Tigers try to tag the Leopards. If you catch a Leopard, that player becomes a Tiger and you become a Leopard.

7. Go back to the start line and play again.

Touch Color

Number of Players: **3 or more**
What You Need: **boundary markers**
Where to Play: **in the yard or at the park**
The Point: **don't get caught**

What You Do

1. Mark a circular boundary in the playing area and pick the first player to be IT. IT stands in the center of the playing area. All of the other players stand in a circle just outside the boundaries.

2. IT calls out a color. Any player wearing that color must run into the playing area. You are safe if you can touch something else in the playing area that is the same color. (Touching other players wearing that color doesn't count.)

3. IT tries to tag any of the players in the playing area. You may not leave the playing area until IT tags someone.

4. When IT tags a player, that person becomes the new IT. IT may not pick the same color more than once, or a color that another IT called.

5. When there are no more single colors left to call, use color combinations, like green and blue, or patterns, like red stripes.

6. The game continues until you run out of colors or energy.

Tracking

Number of Players: **4 to 8**
What You Need: **small stones or twigs**
Where to Play: **at the park**
The Point: **find the other team's home base**

What You Do

1. Divide into two teams and decide which team will track first.

2. The players on the tracking team close their eyes. The other team goes off to find a hiding place.

3. While searching for a place for their home base, the teammates lay a trail of arrows made of the small stones or twigs at 30- to 40-foot intervals. Mark the home base by making four arrows that point at one another.

4. After the team making the home base is done, tell the tracking team.

5. The tracking team tries to find the other team's home base. Get rid of the arrows you find.

6. When home base has been found, the teams switch places, and the game begins again.

Tree Ball

Tree Ball

Number of Players: **3 or more**

What You Need: **trees, soft bouncy ball**

Where to Play: **in the yard or at the park**

The Point: **don't get tagged**

What You Do

1. Pick the first player to be IT. All of the other players pick a tree to be their base. If there are leftover trees, mark them as off limits.

2. IT can throw the ball at other players, aiming below the waist, or try to tag them with it. The other players run from tree to tree, teasing IT. No more than one player is allowed at a tree at one time. If someone comes and steals your tree, you have to go hide behind the tree that person left.

3. If IT tags you with the ball, IT gets your tree and you become IT.

Other Ways to Play

✳ Instead of throwing the ball, IT has to kick the ball at the other players.

✳ When IT shouts "All change," you have to find a different tree to hide behind.

✳ Have one less tree than players so that someone is always looking for a tree.

Tug of War

Number of Players: **6 or more**

What You Need: **boundary markers, sturdy rope (long enough for all the players to hold on to)**

Where to Play: **in the yard, at the park, or at the beach**

The Point: **pull the first player on the opposite team over the middle line**

What You Do

1. Pick the first player to be the referee. Divide into two teams.

2. Mark three lines parallel to one another on the ground, about 7 feet apart. Lay the rope on top of the lines. Put the middle of the rope over the middle line.

3. Line up the teams on either side of the second set of marks so that the players are facing each other about 14 feet apart.

4. Each player holds the rope with both hands. The anchor (the person at the end) can loop the rope under one arm and over his or her shoulder.

5. When the referee says "Go," both teams start pulling the other team toward them. When the first player is pulled across the middle line, the other team wins.

Hints

❈ Have the biggest, strongest person be the anchor at the end of the rope.

Other Ways to Play

❈ All Wet Tug of War: Instead of drawing lines on the ground, put a wading pool in the middle. The first team to get wet loses.

❈ Dirty Tug of War: Play on either side of a mud hole. The first team to get muddy loses.

❈ Tug of War on a Slant: Play on a hill and see how few people it takes to pull the team at the top of the hill to the bottom. Players on the downhill team should switch to the uphill team one at a time until the uphill team has a fighting chance.

❈ Stumped!: Play on two tree stumps, or upside-down milk crates. If you step off your stump, you lose. This works best for smaller groups.

Tunnel Swimming Race

Number of Players: **4 or more**

What You Need: **stopwatch (optional)**

Where to Play: **in the pool**

The Point: **swim underwater**

Tunnel Swimming Race

What You Do

1. All of the players line up in the shallow end of the pool, facing the same direction.

2. Spread your legs as far apart as you can. The player at the back of the line takes a deep breath, dives underwater, and swims through everyone's legs.

3. The player who just swam through the tunnel stands at the front of the line. The player at the back of the line goes next. Continue doing this. You can time how long it takes each person with the stopwatch if you like.

Other Ways to Play

❈ Have the players line up far apart for a hold-your-breath endurance race.

❈ Line up, but not in a straight line. The swimmer has to navigate the course underwater.

Two Square

Number of Players: **2**

What You Need: **chalk, bouncy rubber ball**

Where to Play: **on the sidewalk**

The Point: **get the most points**

What You Do

1. Use the chalk to make a rectangle, 4 feet wide and 8 feet long, on the sidewalk. Divide the rectangle down the middle so you have two 4-foot squares. Each player is responsible for one square.

2. Stand behind your square. Decide who will serve first.

3. To serve the ball, bounce it once in your own square, then hit it into the other player's square.

4. You have one bounce to return the ball. You may move into your square in order to hit it.

5. If you're serving and you miss the ball or hit it out of bounds, the other player gets to serve. If you're not serving and you miss the ball or hit it out of bounds, the server gets a point.

6. The first player to reach 21 wins, but you have to be two points ahead in order to win.

Ultimate Frisbee

Number of Players: **8 or more**

What You Need: **goal line markers, Frisbee**

Where to Play: **at the park**

The Point: **score the most points**

What You Do

1. Mark the goal lines. They should be about 100 feet apart.

2. Divide into two equal teams. Each team should stand behind its goal line.

3. To begin the game, one team throws the Frisbee into the other's end zone (behind the goal line). The other team grabs the Frisbee and passes it back and forth toward the opponent's goal line. You may never ever run (or even move your feet) when you have the Frisbee.

4. If a pass is fumbled or dropped, the other team gets the Frisbee where it landed. You can intercept the Frisbee, but if you fumble the interception, the team that threw the pass gets the Frisbee back. You may guard other players, but under no circumstances are you ever allowed to touch them.

5. To score a point, you must complete a pass to a player on your team who is standing behind the opponent's goal line. The first team to score 21 points wins the game.

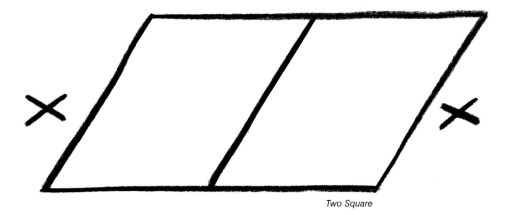

Two Square

Underwater Tag

Number of Players: **3 or more**
What You Need: **nothing**
Where to Play: **in the pool**
The Point: **don't get tagged**

What You Do

1. Choose the first player to be IT.

2. IT swims around and tries to tag the other players. You're safe when you're completely submerged underwater.

3. IT may wait for you to come up for air in order to tag you.

4. Whoever IT tags becomes the new IT.

Underwater Tag

Volleyball

Number of Players: **6 or more**
What You Need: **boundary markers, net, volleyball**
Where to Play: **in the yard or at the park**
The Point: **score the most points**

What You Do

1. Mark the boundaries of the playing area. Each side of the playing area should be between 30 to 60 feet long and 15 to 25 feet wide. Put the net in the middle, between 7 and 9 feet high.

2. Divide into two teams. Each team takes its place on one side of the net. Make two rows, one near the net and the other by the back boundary.

3. To serve the ball, stand in the back corner of your playing area. Punch or hit it over the net to the other side of the court. If the ball goes out of bounds or hits the net, the other team gets to serve.

4. If the serve is successful, the other team can hit it three times before sending it back over the net. The ball may not touch the ground. (You can send it back over the net immediately, but you can't hit it more than three times.)

Volleyball

5. You can hit the ball with any body part but your feet. You may not catch or hold the ball or touch the net.

6. If the team serving hits the ball out of bounds or doesn't return it to the other side of the court in three tries, the other team gets to serve. If the other team makes the error, the team that served gets a point.

7. The first team to score 21 points wins.

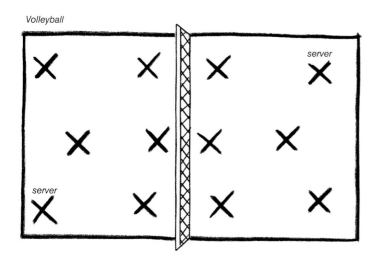

Volleyball

Volleyballoon

Number of Players: **2 or more**
What You Need: **rope or net, balloon**
Where to Play: **in the yard or at the park**
The Point: **don't let the balloon hit the ground**

What You Do

1. Tie the rope or net between two trees (or poles). Blow up the balloon.

2. Divide into two teams, one on each side of the net.

3. Hit the balloon with your hands back and forth across the net. Each team may hit it three times before sending it to the other side. (You can send it back over the net immediately, but you can't hit it more than three times.)

4. If the balloon touches the ground, the other team scores a point.

5. The team with the most points wins.

Other Ways to Play

❉ Don't let the balloon sink below the level of the net.

Walk the Plank

Number of Players: **5 or more**

What You Need: **boundary markers**

Where to Play: **in the yard**

The Point: **walk the plank without getting tagged**

What You Do

1. Set up the boundaries about 10 feet apart. Choose the first player to be the Captain. The Captain stands between the boundaries, with all of the other players on the other side of the first line.

2. The Captain asks one player, "Join the crew or walk the plank?"

3. The player replies, "Join the crew" or "Walk the plank." If you choose to join the crew, go into the middle with the Captain and help catch the other players. If you choose to walk the plank, run to the other line without being tagged by the Captain.

4. If you get caught, go to the middle and join the crew.

5. If you get across without being caught, yell "Overboard" as soon as you cross the line. All of the other players try to run across, trying not to get tagged by the Captain.

6. Tagged players stay in the middle with the Captain and help catch other players. The Captain continues to challenge players until everyone but one player is caught. The last player becomes the new Captain.

Other Ways to Play

❋ Play this game barefoot on a beach so the water's edge is one of the lines. Jump in when you go overboard.

Water Balloon Toss

Number of Players: **2 or more**

What You Need: **lots of water balloons**

Where to Play: **anywhere**

The Point: **see how many times you can pass the balloons before they break**

What You Do

1. Pair up so that each player has a partner. Stand facing your partner, with one of you holding the water balloon.

2. Toss the balloon back and forth. After each successful toss, whoever threw the balloon takes a step backward.

3. When the balloon bursts, get another one and keep going.

Water Balloon Toss

Water Brigade

Number of Players: **4 or more**

What You Need: **wading pool, water, bucket for each team, paper cups**

Where to Play: **in the yard**

The Point: **fill your bucket first**

What You Do

1. Divide into teams. Fill the wading pool with water.

2. Line up the buckets at least 10 feet away from the wading pool. Make sure that all the buckets are the same distance from the wading pool. Assign each team a bucket.

3. Give each player a paper cup.

4. On "go," run to the wading pool and fill your cup with water. Then run to your bucket and dump the water in. All of the other players are doing this too. Keep running back and forth until your team's bucket is full of water.

5. The first team to fill its bucket wins.

Other Ways to Play

❋ Run a relay with the water-filled cups.

❋ Instead of running back and forth, form a line with your team between the wading pool and bucket. Then pass the cups of water from one player to another.

Water Hoops

Number of Players: **2 or more**

What You Need: **two buckets, lots of water balloons**

Where to Play: **in the yard**

The Point: **score as many baskets as possible**

What You Do

1. Divide into two teams. Place the buckets at either end of the playing area. These are the goals.

2. Play basketball with a water balloon. Because you can't dribble (obviously), players are allowed to take only three steps with the balloon before passing or shooting.

3. If you throw a balloon and it breaks, the other team gets the next balloon. If you get your balloon in the bucket, your team scores a point.

4. When the water balloons are gone, the team with the most points wins.

Water Slide

Number of Players: **2 or more**

What You Need: **shower curtain or plastic drop cloth, sprinkler**

Where to Play: **in the yard**

The Point: **go sliding on a summer day**

What You Do

1. Pick out an area in the yard where you want your water slide to be. You can do it on a flat area or going down a hill.

2. Clear the area of any debris, especially rocks and sticks, so that nothing can poke a hole in your water slide (or you). Lay down the shower curtain or drop cloth.

3. Put the sprinkler at one end of the slide and turn it on so that it continuously wets the curtain. (If you're going downhill, make sure it's at the top.)

4. Line up and take turns running through the grass, leaping onto the water slide, and sliding across it.

Water Slide Bowling

Number of Players: **2 or more**

What You Need: **water slide, sprinkler, empty plastic bottles**

Where to Play: **in the yard**

The Point: **knock down as many pins as you can while getting wet**

What You Do

1. Set up the water slide. At the far end, set up the plastic bottles. If you have 10, set them up like bowling pins. If you don't have that many, set them up however you like.

2. Decide what order you'll play in. Get a good running start, then slide down the water slide into the plastic bottles.

3. Count how many plastic bottles you knocked down. Then stand them up for the next player.

4. Keep track of how many plastic bottles you knock down on each turn. The person who knocks down the most wins.

Water Slide Bowling

Water Volleyball

Water Volleyball

Number of Players: **6 or more**
What You Need: **net, volleyball**
Where to Play: **in the pool**
The Point: **score the most points**

What You Do

1. Divide into two teams. Each team takes its place behind the net. Make two rows, one near the net and the other by the back boundary.

2. To serve the ball, you must be in the back corner of your playing area. Punch or hit it over the net to the other side of the court. If the ball goes out of the pool or hits the net, the other team gets to serve.

3. If the serve is successful, the other team has three tries to get it back over the net. The ball cannot hit the water. You can hit the ball with any body part but your feet. You may not catch or hold the ball or touch the net.

4. If the team serving hits the ball out of the pool, lets it land in the water, or doesn't hit it back over the net in three tries, the other team gets to serve. If the other team makes an error, the team that served gets a point.

5. The first team to score 21 points wins.

Watermelon Ball

Number of Players: **4 to 10**

What You Need: **watermelon, petroleum jelly (and permission to use it in the pool)**

Where to Play: **In the pool**

The Point: **push the watermelon to the other side of the pool**

What You Do

1. Cover the watermelon with the petroleum jelly. Let it float in the center of the pool.

2. Divide into two teams. Each team will try to push the watermelon to the opposite side of the pool.

3. On "go," everyone starts pushing. The watermelon must stay in the water the entire time.

4. The first team to push the watermelon to its side twice wins.

Webmaster

Number of Players: **10 or more**

What You Need: **nothing**

Where to Play: **field or court**

The Point: **capture the other player inside the circle**

How to Play

1. Pick the first two players to be the Webmasters. All of the other players stand in a circle. They should leave enough room between each player for another player to pass through.

2. The Webmasters stand in the center of the circle.

3. On "go," the Webmasters run between the standing players, weaving in and out of the circle. Each time a Webmaster passes between two standing players, the players link hands and close up the space between them, so the circle is gradually sewn up. Webmasters can't pass through that space again.

4. The Webmasters try to sew up the circle and capture each other inside. You must watch the other player carefully and calculate your moves.

5. The captured Webmaster joins the circle and chooses a replacement. If the Webmasters are sewn up together, they play again or pick two others.

Watermelon Ball

Werewolf in the Dark

Number of Players: **4 or more**

What You Need: **a dark night, base (a tree works well)**

Where to Play: **in the backyard**

The Point: **don't get caught by the Werewolf**

What You Do

1. Pick the first player to be the Werewolf. The Werewolf stands at the base, touching it. All of the other players gather around.

2. The Werewolf covers his or her eyes and begins the countdown. Count out loud all the hours of the day: one o'clock, two o'clock, etc. Everyone else runs and hides.

3. At midnight, the Werewolf calls out "Midnight!" and goes to search for the other players. The Werewolf tries to tag as many players as possible before they reach the base.

4. The players try to sneak back to the base without being seen or tagged by the Werewolf. As soon as you see the Werewolf, cry "Werewolf in the dark!" This is the signal for all of the players to leave their hiding spaces and run back to the base.

5. Players who get tagged by the Werewolf become Werewolves in the next round. The game continues until only one player has not been caught. This player becomes the next Werewolf.

Wheeled Slalom

Number of Players: **2 or more**

What You Need: **cones, roller skates, scooter, skateboard, bike**

Where to Play: **on the sidewalk or on pavement**

The Point: **navigate the obstacle course**

What You Do

1. Set up the cones in a zigzag course. Agree on how the course will go. Decide what order you'll play in.

2. Each player takes a turn riding through the obstacle course on the roller skates.

3. After each player has taken a turn with the roller skates, continue to go through the obstacle course, using a different vehicle each time.

Other Ways to Play

✳ Use a stopwatch to time how long it takes each player to get through the obstacle course. The person that does it fastest wins.

✳ Instead of cones, use paper bags with sand in the bottom for the obstacles. Give each player several balls. While you ride the obstacle course, try to get the balls in the paper bags. To make this even more challenging, have the other players throw the balls to you while you're navigating the obstacle course.

✳ Put the scooter, skateboard, and bike at various places along the obstacle course. Start out on the roller skates. When you get to a new piece of equipment, pick it up and use it until you come to the next one.

Wheeled Slalom

Whirlpool

Number of Players: **3 or more**
What You Need: **nothing**
Where to Play: **in a pool**
The Point: **create a whirlpool**

What You Do

1. Stand in the shallow end of the pool and join hands in a circle.

2. Start moving slowly in the same direction, going around in a circle.

3. Circle faster and faster until you can feel all the water moving with you.

4. When somebody gives the signal, drop hands and float around in the current.

5. Do it again, but this time, when someone gives the signal, have everybody try walking in the opposite direction, against the current.

Other Ways to Play

✱ Stand in two lines facing each other. Pick the first player to ride the chute. Move your hands and your arms, pushing the water toward the deep end. The first player to ride the chute floats along the current. Then he or she swims back and takes the place of another player.

Wolf and Sheep

Number of Players: **4**
What You Need: **nothing**
Where to Play: **in the backyard**
The Point: **don't let the Wolf eat the Sheep**

What You Do

1. Choose a Wolf, a Sheep, and two Sheepdogs. The Sheep and Sheepdogs join hands, forming a triangle.

2. The Wolf stands outside the group and tries to tag the Sheep. The Sheepdogs spin around, trying to keep the Wolf away from the Sheep. They may not let go of each other's hands.

3. When the Wolf tags the Sheep, the Sheep gets eaten. Change roles and play it again.

Metric Conversions

1 ft = 30 cm	8 ft = 2.4 m
2 ft = 60 cm	9 ft = 2.7 m
3 ft = 90 cm	10 ft = 3 m
4 ft = 1.2 m	20 ft = 6 m
5 ft = 1.5 m	25 ft = 7.5 m
6 ft = 1.8 m	50 ft = 15 m
7 ft = 2.1 m	100 ft = 30 m

To convert feet to centimeters, multiply by 30.

To convert inches to centimeters, multiply by 2.54.

To convert yards to meters, multiply by 0.9.

To convert cups to liters, multiply by 0.24.

Indexes for Games

Games for 2 or more

Acorn Toss, 14; Balance Race, 15; Balancing Act, 16; Ball between the Knees Race, 16; Baseless Baseball, 18; Basketball Games, 19; Beanbag Toss, 22; Bicycle Unrace, 24; Bubble Race, 26; Buried Treasure, 28; Chimp Race, 31; Dizzy Izzy, 35; Fivestones, 41; Flutter Ball, 42; Follow the Leader, 42; Frisbee Golf, 46; Gold Glove, 48; Golf Ball Billiards, 49; The Great Foot Freeze, 50; Hackey Sack, 51; Handball, 52; Hide and Seek, 54; High Fly, 54; Hit the Penny, 55; Hopscotch Games, 56; Jacks, 59; Jump Rope Race, 61; Kicking Off!, 64; Kid Olympics, 67; Lawn Furniture Obstacle Course, 71; Lazy Bikes, 71; Main Karet Gelang, 73; Marble Games, 74; Nine Pins, 78; No-Net Tennis, 79; Pavement Art, 81; Ping Pong Scramble, 82; Polybottles, 84; Random Useless Fact Tag, 86; Sidewalk Golf, 96; Single Jump Rope, 62; Skully, 98; Slap Ball, 100; Sprinkler Games, 103; Standoff, 104; Stoopball, 108; Two Square, 114; Volleyballoon, 117; Water Balloon Toss, 118; Water Hoops, 119; Water Slide, 120; Water Slide Bowling, 120; Wheeled Slalom, 124

Games for 3 to 5 players (or more)

Balloon Blanket Toss, 17; Balls and Caps, 18; Basic Jump Rope, 60; Basketball Court Tag, 22; Behavior Modification, 23; Behind the Curtain, 23; Blind Man's Buff, 24; British Bulldog, 25; Bucket Ball, 27; Bungle Bungle, 27; Catch a Sponge, 30; Clothespins, 32; Cold Potato, 32; Contrary Simon Says, 33; Dodge Ball Games, 36; Double Dutch, 61; Everybody's It, 40; Five Dollars, 40; Flashlight Tag, 41; Four Square, 42; Fox and Geese, 44; Freeze Tag, 44; Frisbee Football, 45; German, 46; Grab Tag, 50; The Grass Is Lava, 50; Hand Tennis, 52; Imitation Jump Rope, 61; Keep Your Eye on the Ball, 64; Kick the Can, 65; Killer Whale, 68; Kings, Queens, Jacks, 68; Knots, 69; La Luna y las Estrellas, 70; Lame Hen, 70; Limbo, 72; Manhunt, 73; Marco Polo, 77; Monkey in the Middle, 77; Mount Ball, 78; Octopus Tag, 80; Outdoor Sculpt It!, 80; Pie Tag, 81; Poison, 82; Poison Ball, 83; Puss in the Corner, 85; Rattlesnake, 86; Red Light, Green Light, 87; Relay Races, 88; Roly Poly, 91; Running Bases, 92; Sardines, 93; Shadow Tag, 94; Shark and Minnows, 94; Sharks and Jets, 95; Single Football, 97; Skip the Rope, 62; Slam Ball, 99; Slow Kid's Revenge, 100; Soft Fuzzy Things of Death, 101; Sponge Tag, 102; Spud, 104; Statues, 105; Still Pond, 107; Tag, 109; Teddy Bear Jump Rope, 63; Touch Color, 111; Tracking, 111; Tree Ball, 112; Tunnel Swimming Race, 113; Underwater Tag, 115; Walk the Plank, 118; Water Brigade, 119; Watermelon Ball, 122; Werewolf in the Dark, 123; Whirlpool, 125; Wolf and Sheep, 125

Games for 6 or more players

Amoeba Tag, 15; Brooklyn Bridge, 25; Capture the Flag, 28; Cat and Mouse, 29; Chair Carry, 31; Crab Soccer, 34; Germs and Doctors, 47; Goal Kickers, 48; Hot Balloons, 58; Kick Ball, 66; Prisoner's Base, 84; Running Across, 92; Safety Tag, 93; Shout Out, 95; Simon Says, 96; Steal the Bacon, 106; Stickball, 106; Sweatshirt Relay, 108; Three-Legged Race, 110; Tiger and Leopard, 111; Tug of War, 112; Ultimate Frisbee, 114; Volleyball, 116; Water Volleyball, 121; Webmaster, 122

Hey Kids! Got a game you'd like to share with us? We want to hear all about it. Send us an e mail at *kids@larkbooks.com*, or send us some snail mail at Kids at Lark, Lark Books, 67 Broadway, Asheville, NC, 28801.